"FOLLOWING OUR OWN NATURE"

"Following our own nature"

Medical Women who started
Ysbyty Glan Clwyd
and Friends

1948-1980

BUDDUG OWEN

362. 109429
Owe

ISBN 978-1-907424-13-7

Printed by Gwasg y Bwthyn, Caernarfon

CONTENTS

DEDICATED

TO

THE MEDICAL WOMEN

who started the NHS hospital service
in this area of North East Wales
prior to opening of
Glan Clwyd District General Hospital

PREFACE

Buddug Owen is a writer and medical doctor who lives in North Wales and has worked there as a consultant anaesthetist. Her book describes the lives of women who were friends and professional colleagues. Most were medical doctors, some having a University training in non-medical subjects, all came from widely different parts of the UK, one from Ghana. All were ambitious and industrious, making the absolute maximum of life's opportunities. All became part of a very closely-knit community in Wales.

The title of book is from a quotation of Elizabeth Blackwell who emigrated from Bristol to the USA in the 19th Century and was the first female medical graduate. The USA has long provided as many examples of female emancipation as it has of female oppression, even misogyny. It was a shock for me to see the final year medical student's photograph of a colleague who graduated from a Southern USA medical school on the late 1960s. There were no female students. As a form of "compensation" the USA is now the home of political correctness and affirmative action.

Female emancipation in British Universities became increasingly well established after the First World War, particularly in Wales, but the strong bias against professional women, particularly in surgery, is only now beginning to disappear. The biographies are widely different in length and content. A common theme is often the huge contribution of the family background to the success of the individual described. Intelligence, determination and a strong spirit of adventure are recurring themes. Many of the individuals described have worked professionally in many different countries.

Despite the almost fanatical bias against women as surgeons, several of the essays describe, remarkably, female consultant surgeons. Common to all is the enormous change in life in Britain over the last 70 years and in particular the lives of those who contributed so much, and so freely, to the hospital community. Dr Owen has preserved a unique collection of fascinating stories describing a bygone age.

It is tempting to speculate how much these stories would differ if the individuals described had been of the opposite gender.

J GARETH JONES
Formerly Professor of Anaesthesia, University of Cambridge

INTRODUCTION

This book records the contribution made by medical women to the development of the hospital service based in Rhyl and St Asaph, from the beginning of the National Health Service on 5th July 1948 until patients were admitted to the first purpose-built District General Hospital in North Wales in 1980 – Glan Clwyd Hospital. It is centred on Rhyl and includes an area roughly from the Dee to the Conwy Rivers and inland to the rural hinterland of Cerrigydrudion. It was administered at first by Clwyd and Deeside Hospital Management Committee which was under the umbrella of the Welsh Regional Hospital Board. The area was supplied with Cottage Hospitals, Maternity Homes and Isolation Hospitals. There were old workhouses, a large North Wales Hospital for Nervous Diseases in Denbigh and two Sanatoria in Llangwyfan and Abergele. General Practitioners carried out surgery in the Cottage Hospitals and visiting surgeons attended from Liverpool, Chester and Manchester.

Some of these women were appointed to Consultant posts, some came when their husbands were appointed Consultants in the area and some, although in their husband's shadow, were able to find a niche to develop their talents and lead fulfilled lives becoming specialists.

Some did not achieve higher qualifications, but were essential to running the service in those early days and had a frustrating time before gaining secure permanent positions. One showed that it was possible when Glan Clwyd opened to become a Consultant

11

elsewhere after continuing periods of training in Liverpool, and one who was a Fellow of the Royal College of Surgeons, almost at the end of her career gained a Consultant session to start a new service.

The first four chapters record the lives of other medical women who have interested me. The last chapter shows how 5 non-medical married women with families found fulfilment in their lives.

All these women show resilience at a period in history when women were escaping from male domination and discovering that they had a voice.

ACKNOWLEDGEMENTS

I have got to know the women portrayed in this book very well, many of whom I have known for almost 50 years, and it is to them I owe the most for talking to me about their lives so freely. Many have since died, but I am indebted to them all for trusting me with this task. Relatives and friends were a great help and they are named in the Reference List.

I am grateful to the Royal Society of Medicine Press, London for permission to include my article on Angharad Guy, the first woman doctor from Aberystwyth. Eryl Smith and her staff in Glan Clwyd Hospital Library have always been helpful and interested, as has Barry Hamilton with photography. Lorraine Orger has coped with typing the manuscript with efficiency and confidentiality.

Special thanks go to Professor Gareth Jones for advice and for writing the Preface – my regret is that I do not attain his high standards, but I am always endeavouring to do so. Gwasg y Bwthyn, Caernarfon have been courteous, cheerful and supportive.

My thanks go to everyone who has helped me to bring this book to fruition and I apologise if I have left anyone out inadvertently. Elwyn my husband has, as always, been my constant support!

Dorothea Caine and her
sisters (left to right:
Dorothea, Ruth, Hannah)
Hannah 1869-1951;
Dorothea 1870-1955;
Ruth 1871-1946

Ceinwen Evans

Chapter One

SETTING THE SCENE

"What special contribution can women make to Medicine? Not blind imitation of men for this would endorse the widespread error that the human race consists chiefly of men. Our duty is loyalty to right and opposition of wrong, in accordance with the essential principle of our own nature."

Elizabeth Blackwell

Women have always cared for the sick and there were some notable women Physicians in antiquity but when the Royal Colleges of Medicine were established some 500 years ago, the Members and Fellows were all men. In 1812 James Barry aged 15 entered the University of Edinburgh to study Medicine, joined the Army and on his death was discovered to be a woman.

The first woman to graduate in Medicine was **Elizabeth Blackwell** [1821-1910] in 1849, one hundred years before me. She was born in Bristol into a wealthy family, her father emigrating to New York. After her father's death Elizabeth and her siblings were forced to find work. She taught Music and then opened a Boarding School in their home with two of her sisters. Later, she decided to study Medicine and applied to 28 Medical Schools before being accepted in Geneva College, New York as a Medical Student, having been accepted by the Medical Students as a joke. On her graduation in 1849 she was top of her class. She visited Britain in 1859 and was accepted on the Medical Register. She inspired **Elizabeth Garrett** (1836-1917) to study Medicine. She was also born into an Evangelical, wealthy business family and in 1860 entered the Middlesex Hospital as a Nurse. In October 1865 she became a Licentiate of the Society of Apothecaries (LSA) and in September 1866 her name was entered on the Medical Register as Elizabeth Garrett LSA. She refused to use the title 'Doctor' until she had her Degree.

Elizabeth Blackwell and Elizabeth Garrett were the only women on the Medical Registrar in Britain until 1877 when they were joined by **Sophia Jex Blake** and three others. In 1880 there were 20 women on the Medical Register including the first Welsh woman **Frances Hoggan** née Morgan, all educated at the London School of Medicine for Women. By 1895 there were 200 women on the Register.

Women's entry into Medicine was slow before World War I, but during that War women took up men's work. After the War when so many men were killed women were encouraged to marry and then stay at home to raise families. In the early 1920's there were marriage bars to prevent women working and by 1926, 75% of Local Authorities used them. Public opinion was also against married women working.

Many Medical Schools had quotas for accepting women as Medical Students until the Sex Discrimination Act of 1975. Now women form the majority of Medical School entrants and it is predicted that by 2013 most General Practitioners will be women as will be the majority of all Doctors by 2017. Women are reaching Consultant status in increasing numbers in all specialities except Surgery and Radiology. Women prefer part-time work which is plannable and patient-orientated. They also prefer flexible working and to have access to affordable child care. They often have unconventional career pathways and are older in competing for senior jobs. Innovative solutions are needed to encourage married women to return to work after they have had their families and they need to have a good work/life balance.

The London School of Medicine in London was an independent Medical School for women and was affiliated to the Royal Free

Hospital as the first Medical School for women. The only other places where women could train in London were Kings College Hospital and University College Hospital which took five female students a year.

The first Degree Ceremony at the University of Wales where medical and surgical degrees were conferred was held in University College Bangor on the 17 July 1924. There were eight Medical Graduates which included three women. Between 1916 and 1931 there were 64 Medical Graduates of the University of Wales with 22 (34%) being women. Many of these women became Missionaries working in the East-India and China.

In December 1923 the first woman Member of the Academic Staff of the Welsh National School of Medicine was appointed. This was **Dr Erie Evans**, who was appointed part-time Lecturer in Venereal Disease with an annual honorarium of £25. She had special responsibility for instructing female students on this topic; this being the only example of segregation of male and female students for teaching in Cardiff. She was the daughter of Dr Griffith Evans (1835-1935) who established the link between micro-organisms and disease. After his death she placed her father's papers in the National Library.

The earliest Medical Woman with connections in Flintshire and Denbighshire, I've discovered to date (2009), is **Dr Dorothea Colman** (née Caine) [1870-1953].

When I was researching the life of Sir Herbert Lewis, Plas Penucha, Caerwys in Flintshire I discovered that his wife's sister had been a Medical Woman. She was Dorothea Caine, the second of three daughters of Walter Sprotson Caine MP and his wife Alice. The Caine family had been heavily involved in the anti-slavery movement on his father's side and his wife's father was a Vicar in the Isle of Man. They had five children, three girls and two boys – one of whom died young. The eldest daughter, Hannah (1869-1951), married J Herbert Roberts who became Lord Clwyd. The second, Dorothea (1870-1953), married Dr Walter S Colman (1864 -   ) in 1898 and the youngest, Ruth (1872-1946), married Sir J Herbert Lewis, was involved in the Arts and Crafts Movement and was a Collector of Welsh Folk Songs.

W S Caine and his family lived at first in Cheshire, where Dorothea was born and where he devoted himself to missionary work. They then moved to live in Liverpool. When he was elected a Liberal MP he moved with his family to live in London, which is where Dorothea studied Medicine and qualified as a Doctor. She became a General Practitioner working in Fareham, Kent. After her marriage, she and Walter had two children – Thomas who became a Vicar in the Norwich Diocese and Jack John.

Dorothea died in a Nursing Home in Abergele in 1953. Her death was announced in the British Medical Journal as of Henlow Vicarage, Bedfordshire, aged 82. What brought her back north to Abergele I don't know. Did she return after she was widowed to live near her two sisters who both died before her? She came from a cultured background where education of girls was important and encouraged.

Dr Ann Ceinwen Evans
[2nd August 1899 – 2nd March 2005]
First Woman Consultant Pathologist in Wales

Ceinwen was brought up in Groeslon, Caernarvon, the daughter of a Marine Engineer, Owen Evans, and his wife Elizabeth. Her father was a close friend of David Lloyd George who, even when he was Prime Minister, would visit the Evans family home in North Wales. Ceinwen had two older brothers; Henry and John Owen and was educated at Caernarvon County School before proceeding to Cardiff to start her medical training.

A Welsh Speaker who learnt to speak English and studied Latin and Greek, she later was the only girl in the sixth form. When young she had Meningitis which left her very hard of hearing and she had difficulty gaining satisfactory aids to assist her disability as well as receiving little sympathy for her predicament.

She had some difficulty in gaining admission to the first year of the medical course in Cardiff, as she had offered Welsh rather than French in her Central Welsh Board senior examination. The Registrar of the University of Wales, Dr Angus had written a letter to the Dean of the Faculty of Medicine supporting her application, pointing out that she was exceptionally good.

In Cardiff she passed her examinations, qualifying in Medicine. Because her disability made general practice unsuitable she decided to pursue research in Cardiff in bacteriology and later in forensic medicine and became a Consultant Pathologist – the first woman to hold such a post in Wales. Her remit was to provide a service in North Wales and she attended the Rhyl Hospitals, the North Wales Hospital Denbigh, Wrexham Maelor Hospital and Caernarvon and Anglesey Hospital, Bangor. She retired in 1962.

She was a charming unmarried lady of fine intellect who always spoke Welsh out of choice. She contributed on her speciality to medical journals, particularly the Lancet. Her last years were spent in Preswylfa Care Home, Rhyl from where she walked into Rhyl and would consult her Bank Manager about her financial affairs who felt she was a strong, independent old lady.

Nerys Harris remembers Dr Ceinwen as an eccentric. She had a flat in the North Wales Hospital and a taxi would take her to Rhyl as she didn't drive a car. She always appeared to be rushing and would come out of the door carrying her shoes. When she died a large box full of shoes was discovered in her possessions. When she bought a new blouse which she liked she would buy another five to make sure she always had one in the colour she wanted; similarly with shoes, she would buy five pairs the same style for comfort.

If anyone touched the doorknob of her flat she would immediately clean it with Lysol. She didn't want anyone to touch her hair as it would immediately need to be washed. She appeared to have a phobia about cleanliness and I wondered whether this stemmed from her childhood memories of meningitis.

Chapter Two

Mary Angharad Guy (née Hughes) [1905-1994]

The First Woman Doctor from Aberystwyth

The parents of Mary Angharad Hughes were Welsh-speaking, Nonconformist, comfortably off, seafaring people from the Aberystwyth area. Her father, Thomas Hughes (1867-1943), was educated at Ardwyn County School. He wanted to be a Doctor but his father died when he was young and his mother was unable to finance a medical education for him, so he trained as a Marine Engineer and qualified in steam, gaining his ticket in Glasgow. He

served in the Merchant Navy during World War I and was on the Archangel when she went to bring gold out of Russia, when he hid his own sovereigns in bars of soap. The convoy got stuck in ice, food supplies dwindled and the men began to starve. The captain ordered the men off the ship in order to build up a head of steam to try to get her out. When this failed, Tom decided on the dangerous manoeuvre of screwing down all the valves to get up a head of steam and the ship broke free of the ice. For this he was awarded a medal for bravery. He was a devout Christian and his ship's company had to sign the "pledge" not to drink alcohol. He was an

Engineer for the Mathias Flagship Company and afterwards served on the town council.

Her mother, Lizzie (1870-1957), was the daughter of Captain Richard Davies (1836-1901) from teulu Sion Dafydd, Borth and his wife Jane Morgan (1835-1897), who had one son and five daughters, Lizzie being the third child. Lizzie was a Feminist, a Liberal, who was strong-willed and believed in equality. She may have belonged to the Suffragette Society in Aberystwyth as her opinions were ahead of her time. She thought smoking a deplorable habit, particularly in women. She met Tom Hughes when she went as a passenger on one of her father's ships to Greece. He was there working on another ship and he proposed to her on the Acropolis.

They married in 1897 at Tabernacl Calvinistic Methodist Chapel in Aberystwyth and lived at first in Bridge Street, one of the richest and most fashionable streets in town. Because Tom was away at sea when his family was growing up, Lizzie had great influence on their three daughters – Gwyneth (1898-1982), Ann Euronwy (1900-1988) and Angharad (1905-1994). The family was unusual in the town as the three girls were encouraged by their parents to go to University.

Gwyneth became a Pharmacist; born 30 May 1898, she married Thomas Ivor Jones on 29 June 1935 in Charing Cross Chapel. They had one daughter, Carys, who married Arwyn Evans, an Orthopaedic Surgeon at Bangor. Gwyneth was educated at Dr Williams' school in Dolgellau and studied Intermediate Chemistry at the University College of Wales, Aberystwyth, before going to Liverpool for one year of Apothecary training. Then she went to London University and trained as a Pharmacist. Following this she gained a post at Dreadnought Hospital, Greenwich, and in the early 1930s planned a new Pharmacy for the Hospital. Sir Edwin Lutyens (1869-1944) was the Architect and he was surprised that her requirements included an empty, undesignated room, which would be needed, she explained, when the Department expanded after 10 years.

Ann Euronwy was born 31 July 1900 and in 1927 married William

J Wright, son of Sir Robert Wright (born 1857), Professor of Agriculture in Glasgow (1899-1911) and Principal of the West of Scotland College of Agriculture (1900-1911). Euronwy and William were students together at the College in Aberystwyth – she obtained a BA and he studied Agriculture. After they married they lived on a farm in North Berwick and had four children.

Angharad, the youngest, was born on 1 March 1905. She was educated at Ardwyn County School, where she became head girl (1922-23). She excelled scholastically and on the sports field as a member of the hockey team. She also had debating skills. In the History of Ardwyn, Lloyd wrote:

No doubt motivated by the General Election of November 1922 which put the Tories in power, the School held a mock-election for the senior pupils. Percy Evans was judged to have made the best electioneering speech and Angharad Hughes dealt with questions most effectively..... Against the National trend Percy Evans (National Liberal) topped the poll with 40 votes against Angharad Hughes (Independent Liberal) 36 votes. Percy Evans and Angharad Hughes had, earlier in the year, been appointed the first ever School Captains.

Angharad was direct and did not suffer fools gladly. She could be scathing and sarcastic, skills perhaps honed in the debating chamber. After leaving Ardwyn with the Headmaster's commendation of tact, loyalty and reliability, Angharad took her first MB at the University College, Aberystwyth and her preclinical studies in Cardiff, gaining a BSc Wales in 1926. Then she went to Charing Cross Medical School in London to do her clinical studies. This was because she knew of the unrest in Cardiff and wanted to be near her sister Gwyneth.

Angharad qualified MRCS LRCP in 1929 and MB BCh in 1933. She had been encouraged by her father to read Medicine to make up for his thwarted ambition. He was extremely proud of her achievement and felt he had achieved his ambition through her. She was fortunate to be chosen to do House jobs with eminent men and to have a good grounding in Medicine and Surgery. Mr Norman

Lake (1888-1966) was a pioneer Gastrectomist; Sir Gordon Holmes (1876-1965) described the Holmes-Adie sign for Syphilis (with Dr W J Adie, 1886-1935). When Angharad left Charing Cross, Mr Lake recommended her very highly and was sure she would bring credit to any institution to which she was appointed. Dr W I Jones, Senior Anaesthetist, said that she had great experience in the administration of Anaesthetics. The Dean of the Medical School stated she was one of the best House Surgeons he had ever had.

After leaving London she spent a year in General Practice in Holmes Chapel, Cheshire, with a Senior Partner who carried out kitchen table surgery whilst she gave the anaesthetic. He was idiosyncratic and would not allow her to drive a car, as he thought it demeaning for a woman. As a consequence, although she held a valid driving licence she never drove but took buses to work. He also scolded her for her misuse of Latin. She had recorded that the patient had complained of passing flatus per urethra – "Per Urethram Mamzell", he said.

She moved to work in the Children's Hospital in Newcastle upon Tyne and then to Edinburgh for a year to the Maternity Hospital run by Elsie Inglis (1864-1917), to be near her fiancé. She had met John Alan Guy in her sister Euronwy's married home in North Berwick. They were engaged for four years before marriage.

After leaving the Elsie Inglis Hospital she worked for a year at the Mental Hospital, Gogarburn, where the same Consultant taught her son when he was a Medical Student at the Hospital.

Joan Rose, Consultant Obstetrician at the Elsie Inglis Hospital, refers to her as a careful observer with sound knowledge of Medicine and Obstetrics, who was thoughtful for her patients, conscientious and thorough in the discharge of her duties. "She has a charming personality and maintains excellent relations with her colleagues".

John Alan Guy (1905-1987), Angharad's husband, was born in Leeds on 12 July 1905. He was educated at the Edinburgh Academy and completed his medical studies in that city. His father, who advised him to work in public health, was also called John Guy (1872-1951) and came from Ayrshire. He was intellectually bright and was admitted to Glasgow Medical School, where he qualified in 1894. He moved to England as a General Practitioner – first to Leeds, where his son John was born, and then to Gloucester – before returning to Edinburgh as Medical Officer of Health for the city. He published a book entitled *Pulmonary Tuberculosis: Its Diagnosis and Treatment* in 1923. At this time he had qualified MD, DPH, FRCP.

John and Angharad were married in Tabernacl Calvinistic Methodist Chapel, Aberystwyth on 5 December 1934 and lived at first in Chester Street, Edinburgh, where their eldest child, Joanna, was born.

Women's entry into Medicine was slow before World War I. During the war, with so many men called up to fight, women took on men's work but after it, as so many men had been killed, women were encouraged to stay at home and have families. In the early 1920s there was widespread introduction of marriage bars to prevent married women working and, by 1926, 75% of local authorities used them. Public opinion was against women working after marriage. When Angharad married she decided the socially correct thing to do was to give up her professional career in order to devote herself to her husband and family. The family moved to Uttoxeter, Staffordshire, where John became an Assistant in General Practice and where their son John Geraint was born. In 1938/9 John became an Assistant Medical Officer of Health in Barrow-in-Furness, where they had a good lifestyle, with maids to help in the home. She and John loved family life and Geraint remembers the first 10 years of his life as blissful and idyllic.

War came and Barrow was bombed. When John was conscripted, Angharad and her children were invited to North Berwick to live with Euronwy for the duration of the war. Just before they arrived, the second enemy bomber brought down in the war landed on their farm and a picture of this appeared on the front page of *Picture Post*.

John joined the Royal Army Medical Corps and was posted to the

Irish Guards in Dover Castle. He did not go overseas but was posted to Cornwall, attached to an air squadron, and then transferred to Barton near Edinburgh, which was closer to his family.

Alison, their youngest child, was born in 1943. Angharad helped on the farm and although invited to help in General Practice, was unable to accept because of her family commitment. Her two oldest children went to school in North Berwick until the war ended and they then returned to live in Barrow.

John became School and County Medical Officer for Westmorland and in 1950 built a house in Kendal, where they remained for the rest of their lives. Kendal was a busy market town of 20,000 persons; it had the lowest unemployment rate in the country. The children attended grammar school in Kendal and Geraint, aged 13, was sent to a boarding school in York, Bootham School. Alison attended the Quaker Sister School and the Mount School in York.

John Guy was an introvert who loved children. Because of the nature of his work in a government post with statutory obligations, they did not mix socially. Doctors who worked in public health tended to be shunned by the local General Practitioners. The former would screen children in clinics at age five, nine and 14 years and, when they diagnosed congenital heart disease, the General Practitioners were incensed as they had missed the condition. It was said this was exacerbated in Kendal by the personalities of the Doctors in the town.

It was 15 years before Angharad returned to professional work, carrying out Anaesthesia for local Dentists for two or three sessions a week. This was a frightening prospect for someone who had not practised Medicine for so long and she did not enjoy it. Later she undertook school and baby clinics; she had a relaxed, encouraging approach to breast-feeding. She enjoyed working with mothers and children and teaching them about hygiene and healthy living. She also gave talks to schools, societies, church socials and the Caledonian Society, and she became involved with the St John

Ambulance Brigade. Her daughter Joanna said she would have made a very good General Practitioner. She did not receive any training but learnt on the job, as was the custom at that time. There was no postgraduate training, and this was typical work for women with children who wanted to practice Medicine.

She was invited to take part in a screening programme for cervical cancer in the early 1960s. A large amount of money had been left to a Trust based in Carlisle to set up a private screening programme and after training she held clinics for this purpose once a month in Kendal.

For the last 20 years of their lives they were self-sufficient, with few close friends. As a Medical Student John had lived and studied at home without a social life; he was a very nice man but not sociable, and difficult to get to know. Angharad was naturally sociable – a twenties flapper who had suppressed this side of her personality. They both loved music and played their grand piano. They walked a lot in their younger days but later she became overweight and took no exercise other than gardening, which she loved, and she grew all her own vegetables. She hated housework but was a very good cook. She liked to go out for a meal but John far preferred to eat at home as he said her cooking was so much better.

She worked until her husband retired late in 1969. In 1976 he had a bad coronary thrombosis, followed by a second in New Zealand in the early 1980s. He became very breathless and she spent the next few years looking after him until his death, following which she supported the British Heart Foundation. After his death she was left comfortably off but, like many old people, she refused to spend her money and would turn off the central heating in order to save the expense. She was determined to keep her independence and her children had to insist she had a home-help and a gardener.

Angharad was gifted and creative artistically in pottery, metal beating, jewellery and painting. She collected antique porcelain and had a great interest in antiques generally. Although not interested in clothes and fashion when she was young, she took care of the way she dressed and was interested in good fabrics, particularly from Liberty in London, and had her clothes made by a good tailoress in Kendal, Miss Jackson. She enjoyed reading, particularly biography and detective stories. She was a member of the Women's Institute (WI) and, as she was interested in the problems faced by Ugandan farmers, she would take weekly orders to bake scones, cakes and biscuits for the WI stall in Kendal market with all proceeds going to help Ugandans.

Interested in her Welsh heritage, she translated from Welsh into English an account of an ancestor's life – the Reverend Richard Hughes, born in 1825, who became Bishop of the West after emigrating with his family to America in 1870. She also carried out research on the Cambrian coasters and was interested in their history.

She was modest, a member of the United Reform Church, who occasionally attended Quaker meetings, so it was not in her nature to promote herself – a fine, multitalented lady who carried out much quiet good, was good company and had a dry sense of humour.

At the end of her life she told one of her grandsons that she had had a successful life – she had had three children, all educated and all three happily married with children of their own. She had encouraged her children when they had educational difficulties and told them "if you want to do something – you will do it". It was an encouraging culture and not a blame one.

Apart from having been treated successfully for uterine cancer and some arthritis, she remained well until the last two months of her life, when she suffered a series of small strokes and after the last refused to eat or drink. She died on 16 September 1994 and her obituary appeared in the British Medical Journal. She was cremated and her ashes placed with John's in Aberlady – a town on the coast between Edinburgh and North Berwick.

All three children went to University: Joanna and Geraint became Doctors and Alison read Spanish and French in Dublin. Each married and had a family.

Joanna lives in New Zealand and married Fridjof Hanson, a Dutch Australian Surgeon whom she met in Edinburgh, where they were both training. They emigrated to New Zealand, where Joanna became a Consultant Anaesthetist, and had two children. Angharad and John visited New Zealand four times and after his death she went once on her own.

John Geraint married Doreen, also a Doctor, and had two children, one of whom became a Radiologist. Geraint became a Consultant Orthopaedic Surgeon but retired early from the National Health Service because of ill health and became Chairman of the charity World Orthopaedic Concern.

Alison married John Wright (unrelated to Euronwy's husband) and had two children, neither of whom studied Medicine. Alison carried out a research project on a seventeenth-century Catholic family to gain a PhD.

Angharad was a woman of outstanding promise who did not fulfil her professional potential. She was bitter that the war had ended a pleasant lifestyle and regretted that she had not taken up General Practice when asked to do so. She had no postgraduate qualifications at the time of her marriage: these would have been useful since she lived in a small market town and not in a city, where she might have had more choice of work and fulfilment. She was a woman who was caught in a social trap and unable to find an outlet for all her talents – a woman before her time.

Permission granted by Royal Society of Medicine Press, London.

Chapter Three

THE FOUR WOMEN IN THIS CHAPTER
HAVE INTERESTED ME FOR
DIFFERENT REASONS

I have included a letter written by Dr Mayer as an example of the peripatetic life lead by a Refugee doctor in the 1930's and 1940's until she found permanent sanctuary as a member of staff in Llangwyfan Sanatorium in the Vale of Clwyd.

Dr Margaret Morgan was born in my home town, Aberystwyth, and her life was altered by Tuberculosis and Depression. She was treated in Llangwyfan Sanatorium for Tuberculosis.

Dr Eirian Hayward (née Thomas) was my best friend when we were both medical students in Cardiff. She returned to medicine after having a family.

Dr Hilary Loxdale (née Steen) interested me through her connection with the London Hospital and Cardiganshire, and being the first medical woman to be a resident House Officer in Bristol.

Dr R Von Stienen Mayer

Resident Medical Officer, Llangwyfan [1943-1962]

This letter is a typed version of a handwritten letter written by Dr Mayer to Dr Biagi, Medical Superintendent, Llangwyfan Hospital giving an account of her life as a Refugee Doctor.

"I was born near Berlin, the fifth of eight brothers and sisters. After a happy childhood I started my training as a Doctor during the first World War, attending the Universities of Berlin, Munich, Jeva and Marburg. I finished my education in 1921 and then I worked at TB Hospitals and, since 1924, at Children's Clinics. In 1928, I was put in charge of a small Children's State Hospital and of the Child Welfare at Gotha – a most rewarding task at the time. But Nazism began in that part of Germany and I resigned my post in 1931. Things deteriorated soon everywhere and I left Germany in 1933 and became partner in the management of a small boarding house in Florence, the finest place to go to – so it seemed to me if I had to leave Germany and give up my home, my profession, my friends and my language.

The beginning was not easy, but gradually my friend and I succeeded to create a kind of refuge to the many who were oppressed by the strangling machinations of Nazism – and life had a new meaning.

Following the visit of Hitler to Mussolini, however, Italy also became forbidden territory, and in 1939 with the help of friends and of others quite unknown to me, I was given the permit to enter Great Britain as a Midwife pupil. This was the only way I was accepted for training at Queen Charlotte's Maternity Hospital, after some difficulties on account of my age were overcome.

The "training" came to an abrupt end in June 1940 (the only time when there was a panic in this country), when all the pupils of enemy-alien origin (there were nine of us at Queen Charlotte's; all Doctors, but one) were, literally put into the ... from one hour to the other. I was fortunate to find a temporary refuge at a cousin of mine who was at the point of leaving to the USA (in six weeks). I then took a room in a house which was evacuated by its owners on account of the blitz and lived on my own with a bank balance of £50 and no permit to work. A friend whom I was to marry was deported to Canada two days before our wedding was due. At the end of 1940, however, I was allowed to do odd nursing jobs – some very odd! and in February 1941 my friend was released. By that time, alien Doctors could obtain temporary registration – but, in my case, the combination of being a woman, German, married and a Paediatrician proved to be an obstacle unconquerable and I applied more than a hundred times for all kinds of M.O. jobs without even getting a single interview.

In November 1942 my husband died – having been ill for more than a year. Renewing my applications for medical work there was no difficulty any more to be accepted and I chose to go to the North Wales Sanatorium, Llangwyfan in early 1943 – where I remained uninterrupted until my retirement in March 1962. I certainly would not have chosen such a career voluntarily – but looking back I feel that my life has been enriched by all those vicissitudes in many ways. The German, the Italian and the English characters are very different – coming to know them intimately and trying to adapt oneself to the demands set by a new language, new professional tasks, new social surroundings and very different traditions and cultures opens one's eyes to one's own shortcomings – and one is given a second chance to learn and to free one's mind from many prejudices. In the end, a great gratitude fills one's heart for all the kindness, understanding, help and encouragement given by many people, for the great experience of getting acquainted with a new literature and with all it expresses and stands for, and, last but not least with the "English way of life", an expression which comprises of a great deal of things.

However, my first thanks go to Llangwyfan, the place as well as those who lived there, for their great share in making me feel that life was worthwhile again."

Margaret Iola Morgan BA, BSc, MB BCh [1916-1976]

I knew Margaret Morgan as a General Practitioner in Aberystwyth who seemed very reserved and distant and who made no attempt to seek me out as a young Medical Student who qualified 2 years after her. She was a town girl and I was a country girl. Her father was a General Practitioner in Aberystwyth, but we didn't attend his Practice, so she was a world away from me. She had straight black cropped hair, walked with a limp and her obituary explained a lot about her.

She was born on the 21 July 1916 and in her youth had been a good athlete with a gift for languages. After a pass degree in German at the University College of Wales, Aberystwyth she prepared for an Honours Degree with a period of study in Düsseldorf. Unfortunately, she developed problems with her hip which necessitated her return home in September 1937 and the following 2 years she spent in the North Wales Sanatorium in Llangwyfan, Denbighshire. This was a time when Dr Fenwick Jones was the Medical Superintendent. She returned home in plaster for the first Christmas of World War II. She decided to change her course, to study Medicine with a view to pursuing a career in the Tuberculosis Service. Firstly, she re-entered Aberystwyth College to do her Intermediate examinations to gain her First MB. A switch from languages to science resulted in her gaining the Dr Thomas Jones Exhibition for the best student undertaking this course of her year. She proceeded to Cardiff to do the Second MB. and then her clinical course in the Welsh National School of Medicine, qualifying in 1947. She graduated in Wales and in London with Honours. Unfortunately, this was followed by depression from which she suffered for the rest of her life. She gave up the idea of pursuing a career in the Tuberculosis Service and instead joined her brother-in-law in her father's old Practice where she remained for the rest of her professional life. She retained an interest in travel, languages, swimming and Red Cross work and after her retirement developed an interest in woodwind instruments and music. She suffered a distressing terminal illness and died in Morriston Hospital aged 60 years. She was said to have lived quietly and unobtrusively. She was obviously a girl of many gifts who was hampered by her illness and disability, but who succeeded with determination to overcome them.

Eirian Hayward BSc, MB BCh, DRCOG
[22nd September 1925 – 16th August 1978]
Senior Medical Officer – Leicester and Leicestershire Health Authority (Teaching)

Eirian was my best friend in Medical School in Cardiff. We met in Aberdare Hall, the Residential Hall for female students in Cathays Park and I became her partner for Anatomy Dissection. She was an ideal partner for this, as she was meticulously tidy and neat in fine work such as needlework and we got on well together.

She was eighteen months or so older than I was and the only child of the Headmaster of Bridgend Grammar School, both parents being elderly when Eirian was born. She had medical connections as two of her father's brothers were well known. Melbourne Thomas was the Medical Superintendent of Church Village Hospital and Dilwyn Thomas was a well-known Chest Physician of Sully Hospital. After we left Aberdare Hall we shared "digs" – firstly in Ladysmith Avenue and then in Cyncoed Road with a widow whose two sons had left home. Mrs Nixon had a very large bungalow and garden in an affluent area of Cardiff. Whilst we were there Eirian developed appendicitis and was anaesthetised by the well-known Anaesthetist Professor W W Mushin when she had her appendix removed.

Eirian Thomas was born on the 22nd September 1925 and educated in Bridgend Grammar School, becoming Head Girl, before proceeding to Cardiff. Her family was musical and Eirian played the Cello to a high standard. It was an artistic home with many paintings – copies of the Dutch Masters hung on the walls in the large rooms in Revidge, Park Street. She had been well taught by her mother in sewing, knitting and cooking and how to keep a clean, tidy house herself. This she took to heart endeavouring to do everything herself when she married instead of getting help and delegating. I think she regarded this as being a good wife following her mother's example.

Eirian and I regularly attended Chamber Music Concerts in the Reardon Smith Hall and we also walked a lot, a hobby we both enjoyed; walking up the Wenallt to have afternoon tea on a Sunday. We also were part of a group of medical students who had a youth hostelling walking holiday in the Forest of Dean.

I met her future husband, Bill Hayward, when he returned from Italy in WWII and was stationed in Bibury in an RAF camp. I was the "gooseberry" who chaperoned her when she visited the camp and we stayed in the guest quarters. Bill was quiet and studious and later went to Cambridge to read History. He had lost his mother at a young age and he and his two brothers were brought up by their father. After we qualified and she had done her House jobs, they married and lived at first in Lincoln where she became a general practitioner and Bill taught history.

They then moved to Wiltshire living in accommodation close to Dauntseys School where, again, Bill taught and was a Housemaster. This proved to be one of the happiest periods of her life, living in the country and making friends who remained close for the rest of her life, even when they all dispersed around the country as jobs arose and promotions beckoned.

The family of four, a son and daughter had been added to the family by then, moved to Coalville when Bill became Headmaster of the Grammar School. For a few years Eirian remained at home looking after the young family and another son was born. When he was a toddler she decided to resume her medical work and recognising that some updating in her medical knowledge was required, undertook retraining courses in London. This proved to be a very enjoyable experience and in the evenings she made good use of the theatres and concert halls in the capital. She then worked part time attending community based paediatric clinics with her youngest in tow who came to know these clinics as "round clinic" or "squash clinic" according to the architecture or the treats on offer.

As the family grew she worked more sessions and became very knowledgeable and proficient dealing with deaf, blind and partially sighted children. She undertook a study of blind and partially sighted children in a special school in South Wales (how they played and communicated with each other and with sighted children) and published her findings. She helped establish the audiology services in Leicestershire.

The establishment of the Faculty of Community Medicine arose in her later clinical life and this was a natural home for recognition of her work and she became a member at its inception in recognition of her work in community paediatrics.

As the family grew Eirian became more involved in the local medical society which held rather nice monthly dinners, with a

35

guest speaker in a local hotel. She found these very stimulating and it was also an opportunity to meet and chat with the local general practitioners and forge links between the community medical service and the local GPs.

She was diagnosed with a brain tumour in the spring of 1978 and died on the 16th August of that year, being nursed until the end by Bill and her children; David, Ceri and Gareth at their home in Coalville.

Following our graduation our paths had deviated but we had kept in touch and later we would go to stay with them twice a year to visit the Royal Shakespeare Company in Stratford and they would visit us to attend the St Asaph International Music Festival.

Eirian set herself very high standards and wanted to be a model wife and mother. She thought she would be taxed when Bill developed Parkinson's Disease but in the end she died before him. She had been a Guide and I, not being one, thought she must have been a very good one. She founded the Girl Guide Local Association (which supports the local Guiding activities) and held numerous sales and garden parties at her home to raise funds. Neat and tidy, as she grew older she didn't mind how she looked and would pull her straight, greying hair back in a rubber band, although she wore good classical clothes. She had humour, a wicked chuckle, lovely smile and was quite intellectual having been brought up in a more structured way by elderly parents who, though loving and caring, were not demonstrative. Her father was austere but her mother was more sociable and a good hostess. I was bridesmaid at their wedding and met all her relations.

It was tragic that she died before Ceri and Gareth married as she would have been delighted with her six grandchildren. She was fortunate that she had found her medical niche in Leicestershire, giving her scope to develop her academic side and carry out research.

She and Bill were not active in the social side of Coalville. He preferred to keep his distance from the parents of the school children, but they had a few trusted friends and attended Chapel in Loughborough.

Her family were vitally important to her and the launch pad from which she pursued her interests. She was happiest when surrounded by her family with her handicrafts and music. She loved walking and the simple things brought great joy such as cooking supper to the sound of curlew in the open air in remote areas of the countryside and moors. She loved her house and garden, which she and Bill designed. A child saying "how pretty" the garden was when on a walk on the adjacent path brought delight and pride and hard work rewarded.

Hilary Kathleen Ross Loxdale (née Steen), BA, MB BS, DOMS [1927 -]

Associate Specialist Ophthalmologist, Bristol and Carmarthen

I became interested in Hilary Loxdale née Steen because as a medical student in the London Hospital she had attended Dr William Evans' Outpatient Department sessions and I wanted to learn more about him.

Dr William Evans' sessions in the Outpatient Department were always well attended as people enjoyed going to hear him. She told me that he was extremely good at handling people and was very shrewd. He would offer patients the best treatment and sometimes the patient would say "I'm not having that Doctor". As there were many patients lined up to see him he would tell them they could go and as they prepared to leave he would say; "I could offer you second best". The reply being; "I'm not having second best, I want the best" and accepted his advice.

She saw a number of patients reconsidering what they'd been told in this fashion. She attended his 90th birthday party and wrote a poem for the occasion, but because someone else had composed a poem she withdrew hers. After Alastair, her husband, retired at 65 they moved to Carmarthen and would visit Dr Evans and his niece, Frances Evans. Dr Evans' wife had died before he moved back to Wales and there were no children of the marriage. She had visited his home in London and she and Alastair also visited Bryndomen, his home outside Tregaron.

She told me the story of when she attended one of his sessions, two American students were present and at the tea at the end of the session the conversation had been so absorbing that one had said "Gee, back home, you would be President of the United States".

He was one of the first to use the ECG and because of this he was invited to accompany Lord Dawson of Penn with his machine to visit a very important person who turned out to be the Prime Minister – Stanley Baldwin. This was at a time of unrest in the country when King George V had died, and Edward VIII had not been crowned. Edward VIII wanted to marry the American divorcée Wallis Simpson. Baldwin was against the marriage but Churchill and others felt he could be King and marry her. There was tremendous pressure on Baldwin to resign because of his health, but Dr William Evans pronounced his heart healthy and told him that he would use his ECG on the cover of his next book as an example of a normal ECG. So Baldwin got his way and the King had to resign. Many politicians never forgave William Evans and Hilary felt that this was the reason Dr Evans did not receive high honour by the Queen for his work as an outstanding teacher of his day. "It was political". She did not think that there was any other reason. I was interested to have had this conversation about Dr William Evans as I have written a short biography of his life and I wasn't sure if there was another reason for his lack of recognition. He wrote poetry and has a book of 41 unpublished poems. He also wrote a book about his grandfather who became a Swagman in Australia for 25 years.

"Need I Ever Retire" was a short leaflet published by the Chest and Heart Association and written by William Evans MD, DSc, FRCP. Inside the front cover there are two short paragraphs about him. Educated at UCW Aberystwyth and the University of London, he became an eminent Cardiologist and a well known Author whose work includes "Disease of the Heart and Arteries", "Cardiology" and "Cardiography and Cardioscopy". He was a Consulting Physician to the Cardiac Department of the London Hospital, the National Heart Hospital and the Institute of Cardiology and Consulting Cardiologist to the Royal Navy.

In this short publication of 24 pages he enunciates pointers for a happy future of activity with rest, developing new interests, how to cope with infirmity, illness and bereavement and how to build a solatarium for the soul to face what lies ahead.

When Hilary was President of the Soroptomists International in Carmarthen she invited him to open a house they had and he gave her a very generous cheque as a donation.

Hilary Loxdale was born in Ilford on 21st November 1927 where her father, Dr James Ross Steen who was a General Practitioner, died when she was 6 years old. Her father's first wife had died and left him with two daughters and one son who became Hilary's step-sisters and a step-brother, a Surgeon. His second wife, Elsie Cecilia Tice had two sons and a younger daughter, Hilary.

Hilary attended a Convent School in Ilford, but after her father died her mother became muddled and offended the Mother Superior and Hilary was removed. She was admitted to Benendon School which she enjoyed very much and in the war was evacuated to the Hotel Bristol in Newquay, Cornwall. She had decided she wanted to become a Doctor aged five, before her father died. She gained a place in Oxford, did one year of Physiology and gained a BA just after the end of the war. She was in the science stream in school and Oxford and then proceeded to the London Hospital, returning to Oxford to sit her exams, and qualified in 1952.

Her first post after qualification was on the Medical Unit with the Professor, which was a plum job. She did two House jobs in the London. She had thought of doing General Practice and decided to do a variety of jobs as preparation for this. She did an Obstetric post in Bristol, followed by a Paediatric Post.

She met Alastair Loxdale at her brother's house in Bristol. Alastair was a General Practitioner there, living in a flat above the Surgery; her future plans changed as she married Alastair and they had three boys.

After deciding not to do General Practice she did two months Locum work in the Eye Hospital and loved it so much that she decided to specialise in Ophthalmology having had encouragement from Mr Garden the Senior Surgeon in Bristol. She was the first woman to be appointed to a House job in Bristol. She went to Moorfields to do a course and returned to Bristol gaining the DOMS. She did not take the FRCS, but eventually became a part-time Associate Specialist in Bristol. She feels she has had an interesting career with good grounding in Medicine, working with eminent men.

Alastair retired aged 65 years and she decided to retire at the same time. They moved to live in her present home in Carmarthen which she feels has been ideal for them. She has carried out Locums in Haverfordwest, Bridgend and then Carmarthen where she worked with Mr Arthur Hayley. She had done Locum GP work as well for short periods.

Alastair died in 2008, but Hilary continues to enjoy the company of friends and trips with the Antiquarian Society and is supported by her loving family to remain in her home.

Chapter Four

THREE FORMIDABLE MARRIED CONSULTANTS

When I arrived in Rhyl in 1955 there were three Medical women who had 1-2 Consultant Sessions in the Hospitals in the area. They were Dr Dorothy Lancaster – Consultant Dermatologist in Caernarvon and Anglesey Hospital, Bangor; Miss Hilary Long – Consultant Surgeon in Llandudno; and Dr Enid Hughes – Consultant Ophthalmologist in Wrexham. They were three formidable married ladies who were married to Medical men and who were certainly able to cope with the male medical domination of that time. I anaesthetised Miss Hilary Long's patients sometimes when she carried out surgery in St Asaph Hospital.

They were of a different era and outlook to mine, but I didn't get to know them well which may have coloured my opinion as they were all well established in their careers and comfortable life styles when I knew them.

Dorothy Lancaster (née Godden) MBBS, MRCS LRCP [-1961] was educated at the London school of Medicine for Women and St Mary's Hospital, London, qualifying MB, BS and MRCS, LRCP in 1926. She spent a year in Vienna studying Dermatology under Professor Oppenheim and also with Dr Kenneth Wills, Bristol. She had House jobs in St Mary's Hospital and Bristol where she had also studied Venereal Diseases. She married Mr Leonard Lancaster in Bangor living in Vron between the old Caernarvon and Anglesey Hospital and the University which at that time was a desirable residence with a lovely garden, although now the house has gone and the garden has become waste ground. Dorothy became responsible for the medical care of University female students.

With the advent of the NHS in 1948 Leonard Lancaster who was a Fellow of the Royal College of Surgeons (FRCS) and had studied in the USA became a Consultant Surgeon in the Caernarvon and Anglesey Hospital, having worked there as an Assistant Surgeon from 1931.

In 1944 Dorothy was appointed Honorary Dermatologist and Honorary Venereologist in 1946 to the C & A Hospital where she remained until her sudden death in 1961. She was the first woman appointed to the Hospital where she founded a new department. Her work covered a wide area as she carried out sessions in Rhyl and adjoining area as well, and at that time she was the only experienced Dermatologist in North Wales.

She has been described as a large bustling lady with a fearsome manner, but who was very good to her patients and took an active part in the civic and social life of Bangor. She was a heavy smoker and hypertensive and died of a heart attack on 7th May 1961 shortly before doing a ward round of her patients.

She had been a keen supporter of the activities of Medical women and an active Member of the Medical Women's Federation being Secretary and President of the North Wales Association. She travelled to meetings of the International Federation of Medical Women in the USA and Canada and spoke at one of their meetings in Italy in 1954 on her speciality. She was interested in the welfare of Nurses and was President of the C & A Branch of the Royal College of Nurses as well as the C & A Hospital Nurses Association. She was Lecturer and Commandant of the Bangor Detachment of the Red Cross and President of the Bangor Inner Wheel and the Soroptomists. An accomplished needlewoman and gardener, she was said to be a delightful companion, a loyal and devoted friend, who kept open house and offered friendship generously. She and Leonard had one son.

Muriel Hilary Eileen Long FRCS, MSc [1906-1984] was born in London and educated in Lewisham Prendergast Grammar School following which she did her medical training in King's College Hospital, London. She gained MB, BS and MRCS, LRCP in 1931. She was appointed House Surgeon to Sir Cecil Wakely and awarded a travelling Scholarship to study in Vienna, Budapest and Berlin for a year. On her return she did further House posts in London, gaining her FRCS in 1934 and an MSc in 1935.

In 1936 she was appointed a Reader in Surgery at Leeds University where she remained until 1939 when she was appointed Professor of Surgery at Lady Hardinge College, New Delhi. However, because of the outbreak of World War II she decided not to take up her appointment and in 1940 she joined the RAMC as a Surgical Specialist, being given the rank of Major. She was drafted to the Military Hospital, Bath where she met her future husband Lieutenant Colonel Knowles Boney, a Consultant Physician in North Wales.

She was then posted to other Military Hospitals, married Boney in 1942 and retired from the Army in 1945. They settled in Llandudno as Hilary was appointed Consultant Surgeon to Llandudno General Hospital with a session in St Asaph General Hospital. She retired in 1967 and in 1972 they moved to live in Malta and then to Guernsey, where Bovey died in 1975, and where she remained until her sudden death at home on 2nd June 1984 aged 78 years. She and Boney had one son and two grandsons.

She had been a Consultant in Wales for 20 years and for 19 years had been the only woman General Surgeon in Wales. She had taken part in Hospital affairs in Gwynedd and had been a highly successful Chairman of the Gwynedd Medical Staff Committee. She had been described as a loyal, kind, warm-hearted, supportive friend who was highly respected, diligent and energetic and gave unfailing service to the area.

Her home and family were her first priority and they were hospitable, generous hosts, although she also had many interests.

She was described as unassuming and gentle, a woman who inspired affection and who had an infectious sense of humour.

I met **Dr Enid Hughes** through MWF meetings, and she seemed a warmer, more friendly woman with an attractive smile.

Enid Annie Ceiriog-Cradle MD, DOMS was born in Penarth, Glamorgan and educated at St Paul's Girls School, Hammersmith proceeding to the London School of Medicine for Women where she graduated MBBS in 1925, gaining MD in 1927.

In 1930 she married Dr Trevor Hughes of Ruthin and in 1932 she joined him in the General Practice of his late father Dr J Medwyn Hughes. They remained in happy partnership for several years and in 1937 she was appointed Medical Officer of Health for the Borough of Ruthin.

She was an accomplished Speaker, interested in medical politics and was for many years an elected Representative for West Denbighshire and Flint Division of the BMA. A Member of the MWF and Council Member for many years, she served on the Cohen Committee on Medical Private Practice and was a Magistrate of the Ruthin Bench until 1971.

She had been interested in Ophthalmology and in 1948 decided to specialise in it, studying at St Paul's Hospital, Liverpool. She gained DOMS in 1950 and soon afterwards was appointed Consultant Ophthalmologist in Wrexham to the War Memorial and Maelor Hospital where she remained until her retirement in 1966. She also visited Ruthin and Denbigh Hospitals and after retirement continued to practice in these two Hospitals where her opinion was sought and valued.

In 1960 she and Trevor moved to live in a large modern house on the outskirts of Ruthin where she remained for the next 26 years, enjoying visits from family and friends, being a generous hostess and keen gardener. She was a Member of the Vale of Clwyd Gardening Club. She loved travel and music, being a Member of Ruthin Music Club and Choral Society and Liverpool Philharmonic Society. She was also a very good Bridge Player.

She and Trevor had four children, a son John who followed his father into General Practice and three daughters; one of whom became a Doctor. They had nine grandchildren.

———

The commencement of the National Health Service on 5th July 1948 helped these three to become Consultants. Two of them had started in General Practice with their husbands and then decided to specialise; the third had been appointed a Professor of Surgery in India but the War made her decide not to proceed and instead she became a high ranking Specialist Officer in the RAMC. Two had travelled to Vienna before the War to study, and consequently the three you could say were intrepid adventurous women. Hilary Long must have been an exceptionally gifted girl to have attained a Chair, she got an MSc for research, became a Fellow of the Royal College of Surgeons and was the only female Consultant General Surgeon in Wales for 19 years – an achievement in itself when even now the number of women who become Consultant Surgeons is low. Enid Hughes had gone to Liverpool to get further training in Ophthalmology and had gained a Diploma in her speciality. Dorothy Lancaster had not attained a Postgraduate Diploma or Degree but she had studied abroad and in Bristol, and she started the Dermatology Department in the Caernarvon and Anglesey Hospital. The three married supportive husbands, had children, and in their day had been leaders in the circles in which they moved. Two of them had joined the Medical Women's Federation (MWF) and had been Council Members where they enjoyed meeting other Medical Women and helping to promote their interests.

Chapter Five

Nancie Isabel Faux FFARCS [1909-1990]
First Whole-Time Consultant Anaesthetist – North Clwyd
[1951-1970]

Nancie Faux told me towards the end of her life that she had been extremely lucky to have had such an interesting life – a professional career, marriage to an internationally renowned Surgeon and mother of four children.

Her husband Ivor Lewis was a man of very strong character, a very dominant alpha-male. Nancie was soft and compliant and some people regarded her as being bullied. Most of the time she was quite happy to let him take the lead and get on with whatever he wanted to do, but if she didn't agree with it she could be quite firm and got her way. She wasn't interested in management and committee work and would allow him to look after her interests which he did superbly well. If a Houseman rang up when she was on duty at night and Ivor answered the phone the Houseman would have a grilling about the patient before he handed her the phone. This attitude didn't endear him to the poor Houseman!

They complimented each other as she was very feminine and

gentle, could appear shy and quiet, humble and retiring and had a wonderful way of putting people at their ease. I liked her very much and it was through her that I came to North Clwyd and stayed here. She and Ivor became family friends and I got to know them well in their home, where Ivor could be domesticated in helping her in the house and entertaining their friends.

She was born in Kingston-on-Thames on 9th April 1909, the third daughter of Joseph Faux and Annie Matthews. Her father taught woodwork and was very proud of his three daughters, encouraging them all to become well educated. They went to Tiffin's School for girls in Kingston which was an excellent school and still to this day compares well in lists of best schools for girls. The three then proceeded to University College London. Nancie graduated MB BS from the Royal Free Medical School for Women in 1934, 70 years or so after the first woman qualified in Medicine. She was the only girl from her year who hadn't attended Public School and she found it strange being called by her surname, as was the habit at Public School for boys. With her first salary after graduation she bought a new coat – her first.

After working in Haslemere Hospital, Surrey, as a Houseman and as a Casualty Officer in Willesden Hospital she got a three year appointment as Resident Anaesthetist at Queen Charlotte's Hospital, where she acquired excellent experience of anaesthetising maternity patients and this was followed by posts in Hull, Fulham and Bow. She then found it difficult to gain a Consultant post – she had gained a Diploma in Anaesthetics and in Public Health, and decided to ask the Medical Women's Federation for help. The Federation had been formed in 1917 to assist women with their careers and in 1942 she gained a Consultant Anaesthetist appointment in the North Middlesex Hospital becoming the Senior Anaesthetist in 1945. In 1893 there were three women Anaesthetists who were members of the Society of Anaesthetists of London and by 1949 there were 97 women Fellows or Members of the Association of Anaesthetists so she had joined quite an exclusive band of women.

When she arrived in the North Middlesex Hospital she asked Ivor Lewis, the Medical Superintendent, if she could go to the Nuffield Department in Oxford for six months to study Anaesthesia for chest diseases. There she was involved in research on the iron lung to treat postoperative chest problems.

When she returned to the North Middlesex she and Ivor got engaged to be married. He was nearing 50 years old, overweight, not handsome and she was a beautiful, unmarried young Doctor. She told me that she loved his wide-ranging interests, his love of poetry, his knowledge of the Arts and his strength of character. In the Autumn of 1944 they married and for their honeymoon they walked on Offa's Dyke.

They started their married life in a modern house on the Hospital campus and had their first three children whilst they were there. Then, in 1951, Ivor decided to return to Wales so that his children could be educated in Welsh culture and way of life. They bought two 200 year old cottages outside St Asaph without electricity or modern conveniences because he wanted the children to experience this old way of Welsh life. Nancie managed superbly, coping with candles, oil lamps, coal fires and a coal-fired Aga stove for cooking for many years.

Their fourth child, Sion, was born in St Asaph and after his birth she had six months off, unlike her previous pregnancies when she returned to work quite quickly. Unlike London when they lived on the Hospital campus, now she was eight miles from Rhyl where there were two hospitals, two miles from St Asaph, eight miles roughly from Abergele and Llangwyfan. Life was different in every way.

She had indifferent household help at the beginning and the children attended the Welsh School in Rhyl. Later the two boys, Gwyn and Sion, entered Llandovery College. The eldest child, Mary, went to Howell's School, Denbigh and Anna to Glan Clwyd Comprehensive School in St Asaph.

Running an Anaesthetic service for scattered Hospitals and night calls also kept her busy and it was challenging. She would have liked to have retired but Ivor wouldn't let her. When he retired he insisted she carried on working and she eventually retired aged 60 years, continuing doing locums until she was 70. She was amazed to discover after she retired how much she missed her professional life.

Ivor's father had died when he was 12 years old and he looked after his widowed mother well and took her on several continental holidays and bought her a house before marrying Nancie. This was probably the reason that he was so keen for Nancie to continue working; in case anything happened to him so that she could support their family.

That Nancie was able to do so much, and turn her hand to anything which needed doing was due to the fact that she was a superb organiser, a homemaker, a gourmet cook and was a mother who had a supportive husband.

She enjoyed visiting different Hospitals and driving through the countryside to work. Anaesthetic practice at that time depended on assessment of patients beforehand by the Houseman and good liaison with the Anaesthetist so that problems were known beforehand and sorted out before the Anaesthetist arrived. She had sound judgement and was highly skilled. She was able to adapt from providing a service in a 1100 bed Hospital to providing a regular service for seven different Hospitals.

Ivor was notoriously thrifty, and therefore Nancie carried out all household decorating, often climbing ladders at dawn to paint the windows outside so that no passers-by would see her. She had a good eye and would mix colours trying to get her own colour for the halls and landings. She was an expert needlewoman who made clothes for the children, and an adventurous cook who could turn grateful patients' gifts of fowl, fish and meat into imaginative dishes without the aid of cookery books.

In 1967 she became the first woman to be elected President of the Society of Anaesthetists of Wales. The Secretary at that time was

Michael Rosen who became the first President of the College of Anaesthetists. The summer meeting that year was in Rotterdam and she conducted the Annual General Meeting in a bus which was being driven through Holland.

She found on retirement that nothing she did matched Medicine for interest, although she enjoyed the arts, literature and music. She joined an Art Class more for the social side than for great skill at painting. She joined the local Embroiders Guild and was a highly skilled needlewoman. She joined the Council for the Preservation of Rural Wales as it was called then (CPRW) and the Historical Society and would enjoy going to their meetings with Ivor.

When the District General Hospital opened in 1980 she became a volunteer with the League of Friends. Helping in the Tea Bar and counting change she found more difficult than being an Anaesthetist, but she enjoyed the social aspect of the work and Hospital.

After they both retired, they enjoyed travelling abroad and later still, taking car trips into the Welsh countryside with picnics and relaxing in quiet spots.

When Ivor became ill she felt the first frightening symptoms of her own illness which distressed her, as she confided in me, but it was some time before they became widely apparent. After Ivor's death she moved from their large family home to a house in St Asaph which she found difficult. She lost her confidence and when she had visitors she, who had been such a superb cook, would ask me how to cook ordinary meals.

She eventually moved to a Nursing Home in Reigate to be near her son, Gwyn and his family, where she died. Unfortunately, due to illness, I was unable to attend her funeral, but we held a memorial service for her later in Glan Clwyd Hospital in which her four children took part.

She was fortunate that she had gained her postgraduate qualifications and a Consultant appointment before she married and had children. She was adaptable and adventurous in leaving

London and moving to North Wales where she made many friends.

I know that she would have liked to retire to devote herself to her family when they were young for she loved children, but in the circumstances she coped with everything and I could not have made a better friend and colleague.

Phillida Mary Frost FRCA [1928 -   ]
Consultant Anaesthetist [1966-1988]

When Phillida was told one day by Dr Cope, the Senior Anaesthetist in University College Hospital London where she was working as a Registrar, that there was a vacancy for an Anaesthetist in the North of Sweden she decided to go there for a year in November 1960. She found herself the only Anaesthetist in the Hospital and worked with Nurse Anaesthetists and enjoyed it. There were two Operating Theatres and she went from one to the other inducing Anaesthesia and leaving the Nurses to maintain it. There were two Nurses per patient, one to ventilate the patient's lungs by hand whilst the other kept the records. The Nurse put up the intravenous infusions. Pentothal and Scoline were available to induce Anaesthesia and drip ether from an Aga Anaesthetic Machine maintained Anaesthesia. Patients received Scoline injections intermittently to keep them paralysed whilst the Nurse ventilated the lungs to keep the patients oxygenated and alive. They were given Omnopon and Scopolamine before Anaesthesia was induced which helped to relieve pain and produce amnesia.

They started work early with a ward round, followed by an operating list at 8:30 am and continued until 3:30 pm when the staff went off to ski, although she didn't do so because in 1945 she had an accident breaking a leg and was in hospital for six months, and after this she decided that she would study Medicine. The Nurses anaesthetised the emergencies which followed the set list. One Surgeon did all the operating. He didn't like Pentothal being used and instead induction of Anaesthesia was carried out with Vinesthene or Ether. An indwelling needle was put in a vein in the hand which could have a drip connected if this was necessary. Nurses took blood for cross-matching in case it was needed and on one occasion it was used. Intravenous infusions were put up in the mornings, fluid given and then taken down later. Relatives nursed the patients post-operatively.

It was there that she saw Spirochaetes under the microscope for the first time in a patient with Syphilis; and Pernicious Anaemia from a worm ingested in raw fish. A lot of Cystoscopies were carried out under low spinals. Fractured femurs were done on the operating table under Local Analgesia which wasn't very good. Tonsillectomy was also carried out under Local Analgesia if they were big adults but if small they were given Ether like a Dental Anaesthetic in the Chair, the mask removed and then the tonsils removed. There was a lot of Gall Bladder and Stomach Ulcer surgery carried out, but she doesn't remember Colon Cancer and presumes these went to bigger centres. Road traffic accidents were common. Black coffee, anchovies and butter formed a major part of the diet and patients had bad teeth. They didn't have much calcium and couldn't get fruit in winter so they were depleted of vitamins.

On her first day she anaesthetised for a Toxic Goitre. After the Surgeon left the Theatre she had to summon him back as after she had removed the tube which was in the windpipe the windpipe had collapsed. This was the only time she ever saw this happen and the Surgeon had to carry out a Tracheostomy.

Another thin patient did not breath at the end of Surgery due to the drug used to produce muscle relaxation and she eventually had to give him increments of Atropine and Prostigmine to reverse the dual block. A man with an enormous hernia, who a Surgeon in Stockholm had refused to treat surgically, had his hernia repaired successfully by them. She went to a meeting of the Scandinavian Anaesthetic Society which was interesting and where an Anaesthetist from Britain with a red face and big handle bar moustache gave a talk.

When she returned to Britain she worked as a Locum in the Brompton Hospital for a month and was told by Dr Lucas, who had Anaesthetic sessions there and at University College Hospital, that there was a vacancy for a job at Great Ormond Street. She worked there for a year or so and then became Senior Registrar between Great Ormond Street and University College Hospital doing a year in one and then the other, that is alternating yearly. Although she enjoyed it she didn't think it was a good job as someone could be appointed at that time who had no experience in Paediatric Anaesthesia. She was on duty all the time in Great Ormond Street, as there was only the Senior Registrar and was allowed off duty on Thursday between 2:00 pm and 10:00 pm – as long as it was convenient to let her have this.

She had met Jean Green when they were both working for their First MB and had kept up her friendship with her over the years. When the Greens had a house-warming party when they moved to live in Coed Duon in Tremeirchion in the Vale of Clwyd, she was invited and stayed with them. There she heard that there was a Consultant vacancy in North Clwyd. Dr Nancie Faux came to see her and she applied for and was successful in gaining the post, starting in 1966. We were fortunate to get a highly skilled Anaesthetist.

When she arrived she stayed first with the Greens, then with me, then got a flat in St Asaph and finally bought a bungalow with a large garden on the banks of the Elwy in St Asaph. She created a beautiful garden growing fruit, vegetables and flowers and having a greenhouse. Although she loved the country she found there wasn't time to enjoy it and could only go for walks occasionally. She was also interested in Ornithology. She felt her contribution was to work to serve the community and with lists and emergencies there was no time off. She stayed for 23 years and retired in 1988 having provided a first class service.

She was interested in record keeping and in equipment. She has thrown away all the records she had kept of her work in Sweden. When she was in University College Hospital she had suggested that the Anaesthetic given to the patient be recorded not just the term General Anaesthesia, but they were offended by her suggestion at that time. She had become interested in the patients who had Cystoscopies under General Anaesthesia and had been given Gallamine (a muscle relaxant) who didn't breath well post-operatively and were discovered to be in incipient renal failure. She also discovered patients who had Laminectomies and had taken Codeine Co for pain who had blood a funny colour due to Methaemoglobinaemia and found a number of patients with this. During the war there were many "blue babies" due to drinking water from wells which had been contaminated with nitrates which had drained from the land.

She hadn't always been interested in collecting equipment, but found that she had to design connectors to connect ventilators to a tracheal tube in the windpipe before the manufacturers started designing them. She enjoyed making lightweight connectors and improvising in this way. She also looked for ways to keep tubes in place by watching how other people did this when babies and small children had cleft palate repairs, to make sure the tube remained secure.

She assembled her own scalp vein needles, and made splints for children's hands by using two padded tongue depressors. Also, they used rubber bands around a baby's head to engorge the veins to make it easier to insert a needle. When she started giving Anaesthetics for Tonsillectomies she used Ether from a bottle –

being dripped on to a face mask until they stopped breathing when the mask was removed and surgery carried out.

She remembers the first heart by-pass surgery being carried out when she started at 8:30 am and finished at 5:30 pm, ventilating the patient by hand the whole time which resulted in blisters on her hand and cuts around her nails due to opening glass bottles of infusion fluid for drips. The grafts leaked because they hadn't been soaked in blood.

At an Association of Anaesthetists Meeting in Bristol, she met the well known Dr Bryn Thomas who had written a textbook on Anaesthetic equipment. She liked equipment because it usually had someone's name attached to it, eg Dennis Brown's Top Hat and Sheila Anderson's Laryngoscope – both of which she used.

She liked keeping equipment and she has catalogued and photographed all the equipment which she kept when hospitals were closing with the opening of Glan Clwyd. She had cards of identification for every item and displayed them in cabinets in the Consultants Sitting Room in Glan Clwyd, in the Postgraduate Education Centre in St Asaph and in the Royal Alexandra Hospital. She made lists of everything and all photographs had the name on the back. This made the basis of an Anaesthetic Museum at the time.

She knew that she didn't want to become a General Practitioner and thought she wouldn't pass the Membership of the Royal College of Physicians examination and didn't know what else to do other than Anaesthesia. She didn't think anyone influenced her in training and she didn't realise that many of the people she worked with in London were eminent. When she asked these eminent Consultants if Registrar problems could be discussed at their meetings, she was told that they did not discuss Registrars or their problems. Nobody helped her and she was never shown anything. She was told to go away during lists and return at 5:00 pm, so she picked up what she could. She said that she learnt "damn all" in training, although the Senior Registrar showed her how to do a Brachial Block to paralyse the arm prior to surgery. When one

Anaesthetist had her back to the Anaesthetic Machine, the Registrar would turn the Oxygen up and the Nitrous Oxide down.

When she arrived in North Wales her past Paediatric experience was invaluable. She enjoyed working with Mr Robert Owen, the Orthopaedic Surgeon who later became Professor of Orthopaedic Surgery in Liverpool, as he operated on babies and children with Orthopaedic problems. She hadn't done any Orthopaedics previously but it was orderly which she liked with things being carried out in the same way and being clean and tidy. It was carried out in a Unit on its own in Abergele Hospital and was a team effort. The Technicians would prepare everything for her before she arrived as they knew exactly what she wanted. She enjoyed anaesthetising the Spina Bifida patients.

The Charnley Tent arrived in Abergele shortly after she did. Robert Owen had been to see Charnley operate and later she went there with Gwyn Evans, the Theatre Superintendent to see him. Charnley had been an Engineer and everything had to be carried out as he said so that it did not bring his technique into disrepute. Written notes were kept outside the Tent as an aide-memoir for the Surgeon. She worked for 10 years with Mr Owen and afterwards with Mr Hubbard.

She also enjoyed anaesthetising six week old babies who had Pyloric Stenosis in the Royal Alexandra Hospital for Mr Jonathan and Mrs Jean Green. Jean Green carried out Hernia repair on children and she and Phillida were a good team.

She was Chairman of the Anaesthetic Division when Glan Clwyd DGH opened and helped to commission the anaesthetic equipment and Operating Theatres for the Hospital. She was President of the Welsh Society of Anaesthetists (1984-1985); was Linkman for the Association of Anaesthetists for many years as well as being the Consultant Representative on the Local Medical Committee, Member of the Postgraduate Committee, Vice-Chairman of the Hospital Medical Staff Committee and a Founder Member of the History of Anaesthesia Society.

Phillida Frost was born on the 10th November 1928 in Ilkeston, Nottinghamshire, a coal mining town where she remembers watching horses pulling the coal carts and where she went to school for a year when she was five. The family then moved to live in Finchley which she liked as it was near Mill Hill and she could walk to school. In 1937 the family moved again to Ilford and she took the entrance examination in 1939 to go to Ilford County School, but war broke out and she was evacuated to St. Ives, Cambridge. There she started in what she called an awful private school but later moved to Huntingdon Grammar School where Oliver Cromwell had gone to school, biking there in summer and going by bus in winter.

As the war seemed to quieten down she returned to Ilford County School, but the "Doodle Bugs" started at the time she was taking her matriculation. When the Headmistress knew the Doodle-Bugs were coming she would blow a whistle, the girls would put down their pens and go to the air-raid shelter. When the danger had passed they would return to the examination room to complete their papers. She passed and returned to the Sixth Form to study Mathematics Pure and Applied, Physics and Chemistry. After deciding on a medical career she changed to study Botany, Zoology, Chemistry and Physics – otherwise she would probably have done teacher training like the rest of her friends.

In 1947 she entered the University of London to take the First MB examination. She didn't have to do Chemistry and Physics as she had already passed them, but had to continue with Botany and Zoology for one year. She qualified from University College Hospital in 1953, not having enjoyed her training but not wanting to give it up either as she had not thought of doing anything other than Medicine. Her father had become ill in 1945, but he carried on working until he was 65 years old.

After qualification she did a medical job in Plumstead Hospital which an Honorary Physician from Guy's Hospital attended. She remembered treating a patient there with steroids for the first time after having had permission from someone from London County

Council who came out to assess the patient first. She remembered an obese woman with swelling of the legs, into which she inserted Southey's Tubes to drain the fluid. A mad diabetic woman was treated with adrenaline to counteract her low blood pressure. Patients with Leukaemia bled and died. The drugs in common use were Digitalis, Mersalyl, Penicillin, Sulphonamides and Amino-phylline. It was here that she had her first salary with which she bought a new pair of shoes and with the second a wireless.

Her next job was House Surgeon in Farnborough Hospital, Kent which was a funny place with prefabricated buildings. Guy's Hospital students were evacuated there during the war. She stayed to do a Paediatric job afterwards for a year with Duncan Leys who was a very well known Paediatrician and a Communist. It was there that she saw a woman Doctor anaesthetising children and she decided she would like to specialise in Anaesthesia. She did a nine month job in the North Middlesex Hospital and her first patient was a child of ten with a fracture in Casualty, and being told by the Surgeon to pour on the Ether. She also gave Nitrous Oxide, Oxygen and Trilene for tooth extraction.

She was appointed Senior House Officer in University College Hospital for a year, following which she gained a Registrar post there. She gained her Diploma in Anaesthetics in 1956 and became a Fellow of the Faculty of Anaesthetists in 1959.

She married Jack Fogg, the Group Pharmacist, in 1974. He unfortunately died in 1981, the same year as her mother and a cousin had died. She retired in 1988.

In July 1994 she moved to live in Devizes Wiltshire, having chosen it by putting a pin on the map. It had a good Museum and the Wiltshire County Library, a good Naturalist Society and Stonehenge was not far away. She already had a summer house on the North Somerset Coast near Dunster, which she had bought some years previously and where she enjoyed going. She told me there was nothing to keep her in North Wales which she had never liked, nor the Welsh. When I pointed out her sister lived in

Rhuddlan and she had many friends, she told me her friends were in the south of England and that is where she wanted to settle. She had worked in the area for 23 years and was held in very high esteem by all who worked with her.

She told me before she left that she hoped to have a long and healthy life and to die quickly. She wanted a quiet life with a garden, flowers and room for her dogs. Although she had been a keen traveller she didn't want to travel in the future or go anywhere and as she doesn't particularly like people she wanted to read biographies and histories. She liked Archaeology and Architecture, but not Music or Art. She had studied C S Lewis, Ruth Pitter and Edith Pargetter and belonged to the Dorothy Sayers Society.

Unfortunately, over the last few years her health has deteriorated.

Patricia Barry FRCA [1943 -   ]
Consultant Anaesthetist – Bangor [1985-2006]
Anaesthetist – Rhyl [1969-1985]

Pat Barry's fragile appearance belies a tremendous determination to succeed, to use all her talents and managerial skill to become a Consultant Anaesthetist and afterwards to overcome visual problems. She has lived a happy fulfilled life – a charmed life she told me, and has been part of the tremendous change that has occurred in women's lives during the 20th Century. Pat would not say she is a Feminist.

Being a long term Member of Amnesty International [AI] and current Secretary of the Colwyn Bay Group has influenced her. Peter Bennison the Lawyer, who founded AI, based it on the idea that the individual could make a difference. To quote Edmund Burke "For evil to flourish it is enough that the good men do nothing". The local groups are gatherings of like-minded people who write letters on behalf of prisoners detained and often mistreated because of their political or cultural views or simply for having offended the powers that be. The Group also lobbies governments and campaigns against discrimination and prejudice. Within the Group individuals take on specific campaigns, for example support for the women of Zimbabwe, campaign to abolish violence against women, and for arms control treaties. Pat has a special interest in East Africa and Tibet.

Having read an article in the *Guardian* by Jean Scott in 1973, Pat decided to form a local Group of "The National Housewives Register". Fifteen local women met in each others houses to discuss and debate things other than domestic and child care issues. It proved a good way of forming friendships and obtaining support. Pat found it difficult as a working woman with a young family to make and nurture individual friends especially with her studies and on-call commitments. Groups offered a way to do this. She feels perhaps she took life a little too seriously and so has a more carefree attitude in retirement. Pat's sister Lesley has moved to Canada and made her life there and until e-mail came on the scene, contact had been intermittent.

"As a female Medic you have to cram in so much, Medicine takes up much of your life". Pat would have liked time for other interests. She has a passion for books and since retirement has joined a Book Group which has expanded her reading horizons. Physical activity includes running, cycling, walking and trekking and before her eye operations, swimming.

She says that she has no aspirations, traumas, disappointments or regrets in her life. Medicine was a career trying to be of use, the caring aspect essentially first and the curing when possible following on. She admits to being competitive, wants to give a good impression and to do as well as possible as a good friend and citizen. She has a strong socialist drive and is aggrieved by injustice. She also has an inquisitive mind "wanting to know".

She gave up attending Quaker meetings because of an inability to believe in God. She can only believe in what she has experienced, not in what has been handed down as doctrine. Now she is an Atheist, a brain centred person who finds she no longer needs an external God. She finds much to agree with in the work of Richard Dawkins. She takes the periodicals, New Internationalist and New Scientist, the latter having many articles on Neuroscience and Psychology.

She is interested in the history of Science, especially that of the nineteenth and early twentieth century. Pat loves the Theatre and Opera, although she is not musical. Opera incorporates most aspects of the arts; spectacle, music and drama.

Although she doesn't think there is a glass ceiling for women in Medicine, she still hears the attitude "find yourself a wealthy husband" or "Nurses looking for a Doctor to marry".

It is important that women develop a sense of self-worth and that the home and child rearing should be a joint responsibility for the parents. Flexible working is helping many women but small businesses may not be able to take on women because of the cost involved. Larger organisations may be better able to absorb the expense of paid maternity leave and arrange "drop in days" to help women to keep up to date and in touch with developments in the work place.

Pat was born in Hereford on the 4th March 1943. Both her parents worked in the Civil Service but were from farming backgrounds in Herefordshire. Nothing is known of her Father's family as he was fostered from a very early age. A school report shows him as Head boy, Captain of football and cricket, position in Class 1. This was not difficult as he was the only scholar in the sixth form at Lady Hawkins' Grammar School, Kington. He died in 2006 aged 92.

Her Grandmother, daughter of a Bank Manager, had a passion for horses. This was one of the attractions for her of Pat's Grandfather who had many enterprises on the go including dairy farming, a farrier's business, cider orchards, and eventually a garage, but there were stresses within the home and Pat's Mother was keen to leave. Financial constraints meant that she could not go to University, so she took and passed the Civil Service examination and was given a post in the Inland Revenue.

When her Father returned from Burma at the end of the war, the family moved frequently which was part of the policy of the Inland Revenue at that time. The start of Pat's sixth form studies found her in Pinner, Middlesex where she studied A level Physics, Chemistry and Zoology. Soon after this they moved to Tavistock, Devon. Having attended co-educational schools, she found Science Masters, competition with boys and an "I'll show them" attitude, a spur to work hard at the Sciences. This was useful grounding for a range of careers. Despite having no Doctors in the family and only a vague notion of what it involved, Pat decided upon Medicine and was accepted to study at Manchester, starting in 1961 and qualifying MB, ChB in 1966. She met Jim her future husband there who was to be a big influence on her life and always supportive even in difficult times.

Jim obtained a teaching post in St Alban's school and Pat followed to do House jobs, some Orthopaedics and Ophthalmology followed by a Senior House Officer and then a Registrar appointment in Anaesthetics. When Jim was asked to go to Rydal School, Colwyn Bay to start an Economics and Politics Department, Pat applied for a Registrar post at Rhyl and was appointed in June 1969. She gained the Diploma in Anaesthetics in November 1968 and her Fellowship in July 1971 at the first attempt. We were very proud of her.

Pat and Jim had three daughters over the next four years. The eldest, Liz, is a Senior Lecturer in English at Warwick University although she is taking a year out to study for an MSc in Psychology.

Liz hopes that her research into various aspects of representation of the human condition in literature (cliché, metaphor, habit and the representation of mental illness in the work of Becket etc) will lead to cross fertilization of the disciplines. Charlotte the second daughter has just presented her parents with their first grandchild – a boy. She teaches English and has also worked in the Education Department at Oxford and on curriculum development. Gwen, the youngest daughter, after a gap year teaching in South Africa studied Anthropology and Development Economics in Edinburgh and SOAS (School of Oriental and African Studies – University of London). She has worked with Christian Aid and is now employed by CAFOD, specialising in Advocacy and Partnership, to produce poverty reduction. She was recently seconded by CAFOD to Ethiopia for two years, but has worked with partners in many other countries in Africa, Cambodia and Timor.

Pat worked part time as a Clinical Assistant for six sessions a week from April 1970, which fitted in well with her family commitments. From 1976 she gained a personal appointment of Medical Assistant in Anaesthesia, increasing her work commitment to eight sessions a week. Her skills and expertise were used during the development of an epidural analgesia and anaesthetic service for maternity patients in the Isolated Obstetric Unit in St Asaph.

When Glan Clwyd District General Hospital opened its doors to patients in 1980, the centralisation of many specialities made it feasible for her to apply for part-time higher professional training and resume further education.

There followed administrative problems as the money to fund part-time posts came from the Welsh Office and the Postgraduate Dean was unwilling to fund Senior Registrar sessions which would involve her working outside Wales. A programme needed to be devised which would allow her to work on secondment for short periods outside Clwyd and the nearest centre where she could get all the experience necessary was Liverpool.

She received Faculty of Anaesthetists and DHSS Manpower approval for seven sessions a week, being the maximum number of sessions permitted under the scheme. Her training programme having been approved, a Senior Registrar Committee was convened by Clwyd Health Authority at which she was successfully appointed. She started her Senior Registrar appointment on 1st June 1981 and was given every support by Professor Utting and his staff in the Anaesthetic Department in Liverpool, and also by Dr Merton Cohen the Regional Educational Advisor. She carried out research, projects and was involved in teaching. She presented papers at medical meetings and gave first aid lectures to the lay public. On top of everything she carried out emergency duties at Glan Clwyd at the weekend every three or four weeks. Jim at this time was also a Housemaster in Rydal School which entailed Pat's support and added duties.

Pat gained a Consultant Anaesthetist appointment in Gwynedd starting in May 1985, with sessions in Llandudno and Bangor. It was a tribute to her organisational skills, keenness, conscientiousness and her husband and family support that she was able to achieve this in what had been a tough four years for them all.

She feels that the mentoring support and help she received was invaluable, as was having a supportive partner and family. It may be an advantage for the partner not to be a doctor as a straw pole in the department in Bangor had indicated that where daughters had a father who was a Doctor they tended to do Medicine, but where their mother was a Doctor they went for other careers. Could that be because they had watched their mothers struggle to balance work and home?

Part-time flexible working is now considered the norm and has been achieved by girls like Pat showing it can be done. Certain Doctors at the time thought that training had to be a full time commitment to get to the top but part-timers pack as much as possible into the available time.

Pat hadn't thought that she would proceed from being a Clinical Assistant until it was pointed out to her that she had a choice and there were people who had faith in her; "Everyone needs a Mentor with a carrot and a stick to spur one on".

Some 15 years ago she started having eye problems and because of this she retired in 2006. The genetic condition Fuch's Epithelial Dystrophy was diagnosed which has become steadily worse. The condition can necessitate Corneal Transplant (being the fifth commonest reason for this operation). After two years and four operations, including one for cataract extraction, there is some improvement.

Pat was interested in the History of Art and took an A level in the subject in 1990 and is now taking a part time four year course for a Foundation Art and Design Degree, which she enjoys enormously despite her failing eyesight. She is now able to see for the first time work she did when her eyesight was at it's worst and is pleasantly surprised. There are all sorts of new lessons to learn when partially sighted, for example, recognition of people may depend on an outline or the way they walk. Steps are easier to negotiate going up, where the rise is more obvious, than down, when the value of marker strips which were absent on the Hospital car park steps in Liverpool at that time, can make a real difference to safety.

She and Jim have been great travellers, walking and trekking widely. They have travelled extensively in Africa climbing Mounts Toubkal and Kilimanjaro. Altogether she has had an interesting life which she has enjoyed and has achieved a great deal under difficult circumstances.

Rubi Alexandra Koyotsu Padi MBBS, DCH [1937-2001]
Associate Specialist in Anaesthesia – Rhyl

Rubi Padi was born in Ghana, died in Johannesburg, South Africa and is buried in St Asaph, the place she had come to regard as her home. She would introduce me as her sister and, or, her mentor depending on the occasion and she left a tremendous impression and gap in the lives of her friends following her sudden death.

In many ways she was larger than life and embraced life with both hands. She had an amazing capacity to undertake projects without giving a thought to hazards or disadvantages she might encounter, but accepted challenges without considering whether they were wise for her. She had the gift of making friendships, had openness and was trusting of human nature. When she was let down she could not understand the pettiness and meanness of spirit involved for she was a giver, helper and carer for all, treating everyone in the same way.

In December 1966 when she arrived in Rhyl for an interview for a Paediatric Post, the Guard said as she got off the train "see you again". On her way back and to the same guard she said "yes – you will see me again", and this part of Wales became her second home. She found there was a lot of clinical work in Rhyl, some quite rare and she undertook a one night in two rota for emergency work which included Medicine as well as Paediatrics, which gave her good grounding in treating children. She was part of a team with Dr Muriel McLean and Dr Anne Sutherland from whom she had excellent teaching and training.

After a year she continued with her training in Paediatrics and Accident and Emergency work in England, including periods in Charing Cross and St George's Teaching Hospital groups in London. She returned to Africa, to Nigeria, in 1976 and realised slowly that a relationship she had there was not right for her and returned to the United Kingdom. Her friend came to Rhyl with her brother on a visit some years later and we liked him. One night they came to have dinner with us and he turned to her and said sadly "You are losing your roots Rubi". He was a highly educated man who got to the height of his profession and she was invited to accompany him to meet Queen Elizabeth II.

She started her anaesthetic career in Rhyl in 1977 as a Junior Anaesthetist. I had told her at her interview to "get yourself right" before she started her appointment as she had had major surgery and needed to be fit before starting a busy appointment. She started as a Senior House Officer in Anaesthesia and ended as an Associate Specialist, retiring at the end of 1996. She had gained a Diploma in Child Health, undertaken training in Family Planning, undertaken sessions for the Blood Transfusion Service and was a Member of BASICS, a medical organisation providing and organising first aid care for emergencies in the community. She did not attain an anaesthetic qualification.

She was a Member of the Obstetric Anaesthetists Association and Society of Anaesthetists of Wales, and kept up to date by attending College meetings and courses. When she later worked in Africa she attended meetings in Durban, the All-African Anaesthetic meeting in Harare and World Congress in Canada, so she had wide knowledge and skills.

Her work was careful and reliable. She was particularly interested in Obstetric Anaesthesia and Analgesia and played an important part in helping to promote epidural analgesia as pain relief in labour and many mothers benefited from her skills. With her background training she was also expert at placing needles in the veins of small babies. She was wonderful with small children both with expertise and winning manner, smile, jokes and sense of fun. For many years she was a reader of the news for "Talking Newspapers for the Blind", resulting in blind people who met her in Hospital recognising her as Rubi not as Dr Padi, the Anaesthetist.

She was conscious in Rhyl that she had received support from medical women and others and was a Member and President of the North Wales Association of the Medical Women's Federation and Member of the National Council. The local Members of the North Wales Association were stunned to hear after she had attended one Council meeting that she had invited them to hold a meeting in Rhyl. All her friends rallied to help her and at short notice a successful visit was arranged with Catrin Williams giving the Hilda Rose Lecture.

She was a Member of Rhyl and District Soroptomist International for many years and President in 1992, when she invited me to respond on behalf of the guests at the annual Dinner when she was President. The Archbishop of Wales, the Most Reverend Alwyn Rice Jones was the Guest Speaker, and the Dinner was also attended by the Right Honourable Sir Anthony Meyer MP. I told them that I had recently attended a Congress in Atlanta, Georgia and on a visit to the Carter Presidential Centre I had noted that one section was devoted to his bid to become President. The three attributes Jimmy Carter wished to project about himself were compassion, ability and determination. These three sum up Rubi for her life was spent serving others, maintaining high ethical standards and working for human rights. She had turned down two offers of marriage but by her example she helped to raise the status of women in Africa and she felt she had shown them that there was another way to live.

She was unwavering in keeping her Christian faith as the guiding principle of her life. She was a Steward, Welcomer and Reader of Evening Prayers at St Asaph Cathedral where she had always been a faithful member. As President of the Soroptomists she wanted her main theme to be friendship and services in the community for care of the elderly – "filling the gaps". During this year money raised was mainly donated to "Crossroads in the Community" – also for the disabled, the League of Friends of Ysbyty Glan Clwyd, Clwyd Red Cross, the Resource Centre for people with disability and to the Rotary to provide spectacles internationally. She supported Aid to Tamil Nadu, India by providing eye drops as prophylactic treatment for infants to prevent blindness.

When the flood disaster hit Towyn/Kinmel Bay in February 1991, she took a week's annual leave to help the victims of the disaster. In 1995 she provided interim medical help for three months in a Refugee Camp for curative care on the Tanzanian Border which received Refugees from Rwanda and Burundi. The camp housed over 106,000 people and here she found her medical priorities changed to keeping people alive; food and sanitation were important for mortality was high. The work was dangerous and they travelled by Armed Guard between their lodgings and the Camp.

For many years she accompanied disabled people to Lourdes in a jumbulance for ACROSS which was hard work and she continued to do this when she was in Africa, coming home for a week to do so.

On her retirement she went to work in St Benedict Hospital, Nongoma, Kwazulu–Natal, South Africa where facilities were very basic and the Intensive Care Unit full of AIDS patients. The St Asaph Parochial Church Council raised £1,500 to buy a Defibrillator as they didn't have one in the hospital. As a gesture of thanks a choir from St Benedict came to the Cathedral to sing, to raise the profile of the problem of AIDS and to bring the beat and rhythm of Africa to St Asaph.

She spanned for us the two cultures so easily. Everyone knew her and she brought with her gaiety, colour, art, music, the rhythm of the dance, warmth, her smile, infectious laughter, repartee and quips to brighten our lives. "In a way she was our Mother Teresa", I was told.

She had a good eye for colour and had a flair for dressing and how to make the most of the clothes she possessed. She attended art classes regularly and took painting holidays with friends.

When she decided to foster an eight year old child she had not appreciated that she would have to curtail her outside activities in order to give him the love, attention and guidance he needed. It was not a happy experience and eventually she realised he would be better being part of a family.

In the Refugee Camp in Tanzania she found Danny, an intelligent boy who had lost everyone and she decided to adopt him. He was sent to Ghana to be looked after by her family and she supported him. He came to her funeral service and spoke warmly and movingly about her – his mother. She had given him hope and support for a better life and education.

One of the most memorable holidays my husband and I had was a visit to South Africa to stay on the coast near Cape Town, where Rubi joined us for a fortnight. She enhanced our visit, particularly in Robben Island and the Cape of Good Hope. On our trip to the Cape she kept saying "I have to keep pinching myself that I am standing here and seeing the two oceans meet" – the Atlantic and the Indian. Our visit to Robben Island was an unforgettable experience to see Nelson Mandela's cell, the quarry where he worked and to shake the hand of our guide who had been on the island with Mandela. To hear him speak of reconciliation and of turning the other cheek to a cruel guard he had met years later in Cape Town showed an ennoblement of spirit.

Some of Rubi's Soroptomist friends visited her in Nongoma and Miss Christine Evans, Consultant Urologist, visited the Hospital to carry out surgical consultation and procedures at Rubi's invitation. Rubi returned to North Wales twice the summer she died before her final journey. The first time was to attend a service in Wrexham Roman Catholic Cathedral when two of her jumbulance friends were honoured and within a short time she was back with the choir from St Benedict.

Rubi's health was not good and I had had foreboding for some time that she was expecting her body to stand up to conditions that would take their toll. When she rang me the Sunday before she died to tell me that she was in Johannesburg with her nephew and his wife, a Cardiologist, and gave me the result of her first tests I knew it was very serious and I told her she must never go back to Nongoma. Within 24 hours she was dead, on the 9th July 2001.

Her brother accompanied her body to Manchester Airport and we escorted her back to Trefnant. Her coffin was made of African hardwood and was the most magnificent I had ever seen. It was overwhelming to think it contained Rubi's body. Her funeral service in St Asaph Cathedral on the 23 July 2001 was conducted by the Reverend Bernard Thomas, Archdeacon in the presence of the former Archbishop of Wales, the Right Reverend Alwyn Rice Jones who gave the commendation. Her coffin was hinged and was opened during the service and towards the end her relatives and friends were invited, if they wished, to file past to view her in magnificent gold and cream attire. A large contingent from Africa attended with the women immaculately dressed in African native dress. She was buried in the new Churchyard in St Asaph where the Africans sang with gusto, many hymns in their native tongue with high clear hard voices.

She was born on the 20th March 1937 the second of seven children, and the second daughter of Isaac Padi, a Head Teacher and Frederica Padi, a Textiles Trader. Her family came from the Eastern Region of Ghana and had a strong ancestry of successful Priests, Christians, Farmers, Teachers and business people.

She was educated at the Premier Secondary School of the then Prince of Wales College now Achimoto School in Ghana – the best education in Ghana at the time – where she showed exceptional talent and gained a Scholarship to proceed to higher education. She arrived in England aged 17 years and studied for her GCSE Advanced Level at the South West Essex Polytechnic before proceeding to Dublin from 1957 – 1963 to study Medicine at the Royal College of Surgeons of Ireland.

Her journey had taken her a long way since her first arrival in Rhyl. Rubi did things in her life most people only dream about. She tried, and if not successful tried again. She went into danger, was afraid, but carried on. A full life indeed.

Dr Eryl Clair Rouse MB BCh, DA
[26th September 1935 – 28th August 2006]
Associate Specialist – Anaesthetist

Eryl Rouse was a married woman, turned 40 years old and wife of a busy General Practitioner in Colwyn Bay, when she decided to explore the possibility of returning to Anaesthesia once her four children were all of school age. She hadn't given anaesthetics following her marriage in 1965 and family commitments, but had started some part-time school medical work when they moved to Hampshire and when they moved to Colwyn Bay in 1971 she had obtained similar work. However, she realised that she wanted to find a niche for herself as an Anaesthetist for that had been her intention before she had her family.

She joined the Women Doctors' Retainer Scheme with two sessions a week in North Clwyd in 1975 and in 1981, after Glan Clwyd Hospital had opened and a demand for further anaesthetic sessions was made, she became a Clinical Assistant with six sessions a week and this was converted to a six session Associate Specialist appointment on a personal basis in 1987. As her circumstances did not permit night work she undertook surgical lists and other duties including the care of patients needing Electro-Convulsive Therapy (ECT) at the North Wales Hospital for Nervous Diseases, Denbigh. Her management skills were used to upgrade the facilities for this unit, to bring it up to modern standards.

These bare bones of her career do not convey the frustrations and delay in gaining her a permanent personal post where her talents could be used and where she had security of tenure.

The Women Doctors' Retainer Scheme was launched on 1st September 1972. This was a new Scheme to help Women Doctors remain in Medicine and was open to women under 55 years of age who were not working regularly, or working for less than three sessions per week. Those who joined the Scheme were given a retainer fee of £50 to help cover their expenses. Finance had to be found firstly from the Welsh Office for the Scheme and later for her personal grading. This was delayed for several years because of Central Manpower Committee's concern that two Consultant posts in Clwyd should be filled first, despite the fact that she had backing from the Welsh Manpower and WCHMS Committees, as her post would not impinge on the Consultant posts in any way. However, her talents gave her a full life of a highly skilled and dedicated Anaesthetist as well as being a gifted home-maker and mother whose children she supported.

She was born on the 26th September 1935 in Llandudno to Idris and Florence Evans and had one younger sister. After attending John Bright's Grammar School, Llandudno she entered the Welsh National School of Medicine (WNSM) in September 1955 and graduated in 1960. At that time the WNSM, unlike other Medical Schools, admitted a greater percentage of women in its annual intake and Eryl was one of 15 female amongst 38 male students. A recent Royal College of Physicians Report suggest 20-25% of medical graduates in the early 1960's were women. Even though outnumbered by the men in her year, Eryl was not the slightest overawed and her quick wit and sharp repartee usually speared any upstart man!

Her wit and wicked sense of humour were put to good use in creating "Anencephalics", the Student Christmas Show in which she starred using her gifts picked up from opera and drama. On one occasion she went to Stratford-Upon-Avon with two friends to see five plays in three days, enjoying Albert Finney and Lawrence Harvey appearing for the first time with the Royal Shakespeare Company.

She was taller than the average Welsh girl, but fine featured with a mobile expressive face which often dissolved in merriment, laughter and giggles. She loved to argue and would often recount tales against herself.

One incident in a Forensic Medicine Viva exemplified this. Eryl was always weight and figure conscious and regularly embarked on diets which made her hypoglycaemic. When she was asked by the examiner how she would resuscitate a drowned person, Eryl being euphoric replied she would use the Ziehl-Neelsen method (used for staining slides to show up Tuberculosis Bacilli), meaning the Holger Nielson method to which the examiner replied "so you would first immerse the patient in acid before immersing them in alcohol". Eryl thought this very funny, but passed the examination.

As well as experimenting with her figure, Eryl would change the colour of her hair and on the first elective visit organised by the Medical School for students to Rome she went with ash blond hair which was a huge success.

After graduation she had House jobs in St David's Hospital, Cardiff and Church Village Hospital where she next became a Senior House Officer Anaesthetist for a year followed by a further year in Southmead Hospital, Bristol before going to Sheffield in 1964 for two years as a Registrar in the United Sheffield Group of Teaching Hospitals, where she met Robert. They married in October 1965, in the days when there were still telegrams to be read out at weddings.

She became a very good, safe and reliable Anaesthetist in Rhyl. She carried out research on a new drug (Propofol) for induction of anaesthesia for ECT, producing a poster demonstration on this work for the Society of Anaesthetists of Wales, who were meeting in Glan Clwyd in 1982. Eryl was also Secretary of the Anaesthetic Division for a while. She could be a reticent, private person who did not promote herself, but her observations were detailed and meticulous, her opinions forthright and trenchant and she was persistent in her beliefs.

She was interested in the Arts, Literature, Music, Drama, Opera and painting. On her retirement in 2000 she was able to develop her talent for form, colour and beauty with the paintbrush and photography. She also attended meetings of the History of Anaesthesia Society.

Unfortunately, Eryl developed cancer and died peacefully at home on the 28th August 2006, having been looked after superbly by Robert and their family, with care administered by their General Practitioner and Community Nurses having been first class. She was very proud of her family and supportive of her children. Stephen works in the Press/Public Relations Department of Cardiff University. Rachel is a Consultant Anaesthetist in Nevill Hall Hospital, Abergavenny. James is an Accountant with Credit Suisse First Boston and Richard a Translator/Interpreter in Berlin.

A highly skilled Anaesthetist she found difficulty in gaining a permanent appointment after having been out of Anaesthesia for 11 years and despite a shortage of junior staff in Rhyl. Her story is another example of the difficulties experienced by married women who move with their husbands and who want to contribute to their speciality in an area such as this.

Chapter Six

Dr Ellen Spiers Emslie FRCP (Ed) [1927 -   ]
First Consultant Dermatologist [1962-1992]

Ellen Emslie is a forthright Yorkshire woman who is always immaculately dressed and groomed, has a wide circle of friends and has led an active, fulfilling life. She was always good at presenting herself with colour, fashion and style, with never a hair out of place.

She has no regrets on her decision to follow a career in Medicine and would not have preferred another career. She did not make a conscious decision not to get married, and her sisters children have provided the family life she otherwise might have had and she has also always been interested in her colleagues' families. She has no strong views on the dilemma of marriage and family life for medical women. If women want both she doesn't see any reason why they shouldn't have it. She does not feel there is a glass ceiling - "get on with it" was her philosophy, as if one is capable one can do it.

She has not had long-standing attachments, although she and her friend, Dr Muriel Hughes, took holidays overseas together for many years. She pointed out to me that all Muriel's sisters' family were medical women, all being sensible, sane, well balanced human beings.

Her parents were the greatest influence on her life. Her father was affectionate, although strict, encouraging his children to "try this" in a no nonsense way, and to be artistic. Her mother was practical and they were all taught to cook and do simple dressmaking such as stitching hems from an early age.

When she went to Leeds for an interview her father had been requested to take her and to explain why he thought Ellen should do Medicine. Ellen had done well in school and thought her Chemistry Master had spotted her scientific interest. He was a fatherly type who was great fun and he had encouraged her. Her father thought Medicine was a special career and she would gain benefit by doing it even though he only had a small salary.

Her paternal grandfather came from Aberdeen where Emslie is a common name. She never knew him but thinks he did the wrought iron gates for Balmoral Castle. Her father, Arthur Emslie, attended evening classes at the College of Art in Aberdeen, the family being unable to afford the fees of a full time student. He enlisted in the "Kings Own Scottish Borderers" at the onset of World War I and remained with the Regiment as the army of occupation in Egypt and on demobilisation was a First Lieutenant.

Her maternal grandfather was a farmer in Northern Ireland, just north of the border, who also bred horses. When her mother left school she did not want to farm and her father sent her to a finishing school in Belfast where she learnt domestic science, needlework and dressmaking and became a very good dressmaker and superb cook, skills she passed on to Ellen. The "wanderlust" was in her and she got a job as Assistant Manageress in a restaurant attached to a Gaumont Cinema in Manchester, which was followed by becoming Manageress of a group of restaurants attached to cinemas around Halifax, where she met her future husband. He had got a job as a lithographic artist in a printing works in Halifax preparing brochures.

Her mother gave up her work when she married and had her family of three daughters and she also adopted an 11 month old baby, Ishrel, born out of wedlock by her sister, so the four girls were brought up together and treated in the same manner. Ellen's youngest sister, Christine, became a nurse and died three years ago. Her middle sister, Ishbel, went to Catering College – South West Essex Technical College – in 1948/49 where she met her husband on the same course and they later opened a restaurant together in the Birmingham area.

Ellen was the eldest daughter and went to school in Halifax where they lived but in 1938 they moved to Bawtry, South Yorkshire, which is south of Doncaster on the A1. Her mother had been left a legacy by her mother and with this she opened a restaurant in Bawtry.

In 1939 her father, Arthur Emslie, was enlisted back into the Army six months before the war started as he had been in the Territorial Army and Ellen as the eldest child, aged 12 years, helped her mother by being in charge of the cash desk and doing her home-work at the same time, just 9 months after the acquisition of the restaurant. Bawtry was on the border of Yorkshire and Lincolnshire, where there were a lot of aerodromes in the vicinity, including Bawtry Hall which belonged to Lord Halifax which became the Headquarters of Bomber Command, and only closed some five or six years ago.

On the opposite side of the road to the restaurant was a working man's club which was commandeered by the Military for Army Traffic Police. So there was no shortage of airmen to be fed in the restaurant and because of this they were given special rations so during the war the family did not experience starvation. The restaurant became a hive of activity, preparing and serving meals between 6 and 7 pm for the airmen who would be going flying later – many not to return. As she said "they saw life"; learnt to cope with all sorts of people and learnt about finance. It was first hand extra-curricular education in its widest sense. She also had to supervise getting the younger children to bed. It was all quite hectic but none of them would have missed the interest and friendliness of the people around.

Ellen's experience during the war of seeing young men coming into the Restaurant, then going flying and not returning had an affect on her. She learnt how to cope and said she was brought up in the school of common sense, to stand on her own feet no matter what the problem was. "It doesn't matter what it is – do it if you want to: there is no point in kicking and screaming".

She had been interested in and good in science in school and there were a lot of nurses in the family, but her father told her to aim for medicine. At the age of 15 she was encouraged to take this course by her parents, nursing Aunts and the Headmaster of her School. She left school aged 19 years old, as she had to wait a year because of ex-servicemen returning to the University, gaining a better Higher School Certificate which she said was a good final year.

She went to Leeds in 1946 and qualified in 1952. She felt Leeds Medical School was first class. She loved her time there, having three years in a Hall of Residence and the following three years in a flat. She then became a Gynaecology House Surgeon for six months, followed by six months Obstetrics which she had enjoyed very much as a student and wondered if she should make it her professional life. She had been allowed to undertake minor operations as a House Surgeon, which does not happen now. She knew that she needed to become a House Physician, but in 1953 all junior jobs started on the 1st January or 1st August and she was lucky to get a job in Lambeth Hospital, London which she thought a ghastly place but where she did well and was asked to stay on for a further six months.

At Lambeth her job was in General Medicine with some Dermatology which she had enjoyed during her fifth year of training and in which she gained more experience doing a Houseman's locum and she decided to specialise in Dermatology not Obstetrics. This was partly influenced as well by the fact that she didn't like the female Obstetrician in Lambeth and got on well with the Dermatologists. Lambeth Hospital was attached to St Thomas' Hospital and the Dermatologists attended both with Dr Dowling as the Chief. She applied for a Senior House Officer post in the department and after an interview she was appointed to St John's Hospital for Diseases of the Skin for a year, as Senior House Officer, where she could study for her MRCP. This was followed by a Registrar appointment in Dermatology in Sheffield Royal Infirmary to continue her studies and then she became a Resident Medical Officer in Sheffield City General Hospital where she got her MRCP in 1958. Following the advice of the Senior Consultants with whom she had worked she became a Senior Registrar in Dermatology in Birmingham, followed by a Senior Registrar appointment in Kings College Hospital for 18 months, where her Consultant (Dr David Williams, who came from Anglesey) advised her to apply for a Consultant post in North Wales despite being non-Welsh speaking. Dr Dorothy Lancaster, the previous Dermatologist had died a year previously and the service had been kept going by General Practitioners – Dr Jack Lloyd Lewis in Bangor and Dr Ian Lynch in Rhyl with help from a retired Consultant in the Conwy Valley and Dr Aileen Hampton as Clinical Assistant who, when Dr Emslie arrived on the 1st January 1962, came to introduce herself and announced she was leaving.

The appointment was divided between Bangor and Rhyl. Tuesday and Thursday were spent in Bangor; Wednesday and Friday afternoons in Rhyl and Colwyn Bay on Monday afternoon. She quickly realised that this pattern did not suit her and changed it but knew she would not be able to do anything radical until Dr Beer was appointed to Bangor 4 years later and her job was split. He looked after Gwynedd and she did Clwyd North. Dr Netta Hay from Liverpool went to Wrexham. She had no assistance from anyone with training in dermatology, carried out clinics in Rhyl and had beds (4-5) in Dr G H T Lloyd's Ward in HM Stanley Hospital.

From 1962-1965 she covered the Bangor area as well. Afterwards, until she retired, she was in the Rhyl area plus Llandudno.

She enjoyed teaching very much and five of her junior staff went on to become Consultants including Dr Richard Williams who is now the Senior Dermatologist in Glan Clwyd. One became a Staff Grade Doctor and others General Practitioners, with an interest in dermatology. She was involved with postgraduate education – representing her speciality on the Postgraduate Board, becoming Secretary and later Chairman for three years, working closely with Dr Charles Hilton Jones as her Secretary and having the benefit of two experienced Administrators, Norah Perkins followed by Gwyneth Stringfellow. She also became Secretary and Chairman of the Hospital Medical Staff Committee. She was elected President of the North of England Dermatological Society. Because she said it wasn't possible for her to attend meetings in the far South West of the country, she was allowed to attend those in the North of England where she was already a member and able to apply to have her expenses reimbursed. She was a long-standing member of the UK Dermatological Travelling Club, the Dowling Club, which she enjoyed as this gave her the opportunity to travel widely. At one time she attended frequent meetings in London to do with Dermatology and was very highly regarded in her field.

Ellen enjoyed yearly skiing holidays and was a good hockey player, but they did not play tennis in school because they weren't allowed to tarmac the tennis courts during the war, neither did she have an opportunity to swim as the local swimming pools were closed.

She did not have dreams about her life, neither did she have big traumas or disappointments. The manufacturing of food and dishes excited her and makes her tick. She was given a lot of information from her sister which she would then try at home. Although she enjoyed concocting special dishes, she prefers plain English cooking and always eats a decent meal daily. Her mother was wonderful at making superb meals with very little. Ellen has always had great pleasure in her garden and is a knowledgeable plantswoman. In the past she also enjoyed needlework.

Since her retirement she has experienced many Orthopaedic problems which have curtailed her activities. When I commiserated with her about her disability, she said "I'm not ill; it's just a nuisance". She has been a great traveller of the world, has given Papers on her speciality in several countries but for the last five years her mobility has been curtailed. She has supported the British Medical Association and Royal Medical Benevolent Fund, but not the Medical Women's Federation believing there was no need for it. She attended the Colwyn Branch of the Council for the Protection of Rural Wales and enjoyed attending concerts. She has been perfectly capable of "standing on her own two feet".

Chapter Seven

Catrin Mary Williams FRCS (Ed) [1921-1998]
The First Consultant ENT Surgeon – North Wales

I was working mainly in St Asaph General Hospital in 1956 anaesthetising for the specialities, at that time Oral Surgery and Ophthalmology, Obstetrics and Gynaecology, with the prospect of an Ear, Nose and Throat (ENT) Surgeon being appointed soon. The Oral Surgeon was full of ideas for the future and of how he and this Surgeon would work together. Then, consternation, a woman had been appointed by the Welsh Regional Hospital Board. It was a disaster in the men's eyes, although they knew nothing about her. Many ex-servicemen had come to work in North Clwyd after the war. They wanted to build a first class medical service for the people of the area. The thought of having a woman ENT Surgeon had never occurred to them. ENT surgery was carried out by visiting Surgeons in Cottage Hospitals so this new appointment was crucial for developing ENT services for the future.

Catrin Williams arrived in 1956 and I anaesthetised for one of her operating lists for the next 30 years. She was not a wilting violet, quite the contrary, she kept her own counsel and ploughed her own furrow. We were both Welsh speakers with family links to Cardiganshire and her mother knew my parents, so it was a good start. I think she preferred male Anaesthetists: Dr Goronwy Owen was followed by Dr Andrew Wadon and she was fond of them both, although Dr Wadon who was an excellent Anaesthetist, she told me, failed to pass a tube into her windpipe. She was what is called "a difficult intubation".

She could look forbidding and rarely bothered with her appearance, due probably to poor vision when not wearing her spectacles. She liked good quality clothes and enjoyed her mink coat but was not a clothes horse. I recall her turning up for a formal medical staff dinner, having had what appeared to be a make-over. She wore a figure-hugging evening dress (and she had a good figure), her hair coiffed and wearing make up which she rarely used; she looked stunning. She had charm, a sense of humour, a twinkle in her small eyes and she liked men's company.

Operating days started with a coffee on arrival and she smoked a cigarette. Goronwy Owen was also a smoker and when he did the list a fug of smoke would emanate from the changing room as they both puffed away. She smoked 40 cigarettes a day for 50 years. Mr Lancaster who delivered papers to the Hospital would put a packet of 20 cigarettes in a biscuit tin in Sisters Office every day, which she had nearly finished when she went home where she had another packet. One of the first things she asked me in the morning or during meetings in a gruff stage-whisper was "well, what's new?" A useless question as she knew better than I did what was going on. She had a booming, penetrating voice, so no-one had any difficulty hearing and listening to her which was an added attribute for dealing with her deaf patients.

She was good with children and an expert on Guillotine Tonsillectomy, an operation now relegated to history. There had to be good liaison between Surgeon and Anaesthetist for this to be successful as the child did not have a tube passed into his/her windpipe beforehand so speed was of the essence. Then the child woke up quickly, cried, went back to sleep and when awake was given jelly and ice cream which they managed to swallow. Pain after tonsillectomy was much less with this method but there was a slight risk of bleeding afterwards, necessitating a return to the Theatre and another anaesthetic in order to tie the bleeding point. Nowadays all patients are intubated and the tonsils dissected out. In those early days the lists for the morning would be 15-20 patients with children having guillotines being operated on first. Getting through a list was a team effort.

She was the sole Consultant running her Department for 25 years but was joined by Dr Narain in 1966 as an Assistant and Mr Z Hammad as Consultant in 1981. Catrin carried out the first Laryngectomy in North Wales in St Asaph. This was the removal of the voice box for Cancer of the Larynx. These were carried out on a Saturday morning, so as not to overrun the normal list. In those days no-one minded working on a Saturday or Sunday and the whole team worked well together, with Sister Dilys Roberts, the Senior Theatre Sister in control, calm and helpful. Nowadays, this operation isn't carried out so often as the first line treatment is Chemotherapy and Radiotherapy and Laryngectomy is kept for those patients where initial treatment has failed. She carried out over 100 Laryngectomies, many of these patients being frail and elderly. One had a Laryngectomy when he was 85 years old and lived to 105 years, dying in 1996. This was Mr Harry Hurst who had survived two world wars. She set up the first Laryngectomy Club in Wales in 1974 and was it's President and sat on the Committee of the National Association of Laryngectomy Clubs. The Laryngectomy Club was a self-help group of patients who supported each other. Major Philpott was the star patient as he learnt to speak so well under Mrs Ward, the Speech Therapist's, tuition.

Catrin started the Audiometry Department in 1966 in rooms under the arches at the front of HM Stanley Hospital with Mr Collier, who started doing Audiograms and providing NHS Hearing Aids. Clive Sparks joined him in the late 1970's as an MSc

Student from Salford University and gained a Degree in Audiology. After qualifying he joined Mr Collier at St Asaph. When Glan Clwyd Hospital opened the department moved there and Mr Collier retired in 1982 leaving Clive in sole charge. He was an Audiological Scientist and he expanded the service to do newer testing. Catrin and Dr Sally Mincsum, a Community Paediatrician started a combined clinic where all deaf children from the county were assessed in consultation with Rodri Eckley, teacher for the deaf and Clive Sparks. This was the only clinic providing this service in North Wales where decisions were taken on the future education of these children, in collaboration with the School for the Deaf in Mold which accepted pupils from all over North Wales. They were doing this before the Department moved to Glan Clwyd. Now Clive Sparks is a Consultant Audiological Scientist and has three other Scientists working with him in the Department which is in the forefront in Audiology in the country.

Following her retirement she became Vice-Chairman and later Chairman and then President of the National Meniéres Society and Chairman of the Wales Council for the Deaf, being their Representative on the Royal National Institute for the Deaf (RNID), and becoming Chairman of their Communications and Medical Sub-Committee following which she was made an Elected Trustee of the RNID. Through this she became a member of the Executive Committee of Wales Council for the Disabled, now called Disability Wales. It was through being the Welsh Representative on the RNID that she met Mrs Marie Noble, the President of Meniéres Society at the time, that she decided she would start a North Wales Meniéres Group and she became President of the Society in 1985. This is the only self-help group in North Wales and is still functioning, drawing members from all over North Wales. They meet once a month in the Board Room at HM Stanley Hospital. Meniéres Disease is recurrent attacks of giddiness with or without tinnitus and is very disabling.

Dr Narain would take Catrin to meetings in a wheelchair towards the end of her life. Dr Narain had gone to see his old chief in Stoke on Trent before applying for his post and had been told of Catrin. "That dynamo: that mad Welsh woman: you'll be alright". She was interested in medical politics from the beginning, perhaps due to her father's influence as she certainly adored him. Catrin was the daughter of Alderman Richard Williams (1897-1966) and Margaret Jane Williams (1896-1986) née Jones.

Her father was the eldest of three brothers all of whom followed in their father's footsteps working partly in farming but mainly in the local granite quarries in the Llithfaen area of the Lleyn Peninsula. In his late teens Richard moved to work in South Wales. The reason for this isn't clear but his mother Catherine died in 1918 and his two younger brothers were sent to live with their grandmother. Conscription had started in 1916 and Richard moved to work in the coal mining area of East Glamorgan. He married Margaret Jane on 22nd July 1920 and settled in Caerphilly. Catrin was born on 19th May 1921 in The Rhondda Registry area. A second child, Lewis Aled, was born on 25th November 1923. They attended Sunday School at Towyn Chapel, Caerphilly and had success in exams in Sunday School. Aled gained a first class certificate on 20th March and 16 days later died of Meningitis at the age of seven years. His grave contains the inscription "Er cof annwyl am blant Richard a Margaret Williams". Catrin was Rhesus Negative and this inscription suggests there were later children who died and she was the only surviving child. Not long after that the family moved back to the Pwllheli area where Catrin attended Troed yr Allt Primary School. The death of her brother had a profound affect on her and she decided to work hard and became a Doctor. She was serious and diligent and did well in her examinations, also becoming Head Girl of Pwllheli County School.

Her father took up insurance work on return to Pwllheli and became very active in the Socialist Movement. He became a Town Councillor and an Election Agent for Mr Goronwy Roberts MP – the MP for the constituency. He was elected Mayor three times and an

Alderman in 1955. He died in November 1966 aged 69 years and was cremated at Colwyn Bay.

Margaret, his widow, was the sixth of 15 children born to Lewis and Mary Anne Jones. Twelve of their children were born at Penybryn Farm situated on the slopes overlooking the Dyfi Valley near Eglwysfach. They then moved to farm in Llanilar. Catrin's grandmother, Mary Anne, wrote poetry and this gift was inherited by one of her children, Benjamin. Margaret lived to be nearly 92.

Catrin went to the Welsh National School of Medicine in Cardiff, gained a BSc in 1942 and qualified in 1945. She gained FRCS (Ed) in 1948 and worked in Southend and Cambridge before returning to Wales as Senior Registrar in Cardiff and Swansea. When she came to North Wales she held outpatient clinics in Holywell, Colwyn Bay and St Asaph and had her inpatient beds in St Asaph.

Hospital politics, The British Medical Association, Medical Women's Federation and Y Gymdeithas Feddygol all took her interest and commitment. She chaired the Hospital Medical Staff Committee, was a Member and Chaired the District Medical Committee in the 1970's and was a Member of Clwyd Medical Committee. She was a Consultant Member of Denbighshire and Flintshire Local Medical Committee. Also a Member of the Postgraduate Medical Committee of Glan Clwyd Hospital and a Member of Wales Postgraduate Dean's Review Committee.

Issues were important, and it was the Medical Women's Federation which became her main focus of interest. She was introduced to it by Dr Dorothy Lancaster, Consultant Dermatologist in Bangor in 1959. Dr Lancaster was Chairman of the North Wales Association of the MWF and a Council Member and in no time she recruited Catrin to join her in Council and they went together to the meetings until she retired when Dr Muriel Hughes was elected by the Association to take her place. Muriel and Catrin were Council Members together for 10 years until it was decided that there should be a time limit for Council membership.

I interviewed Catrin in 1996 and she told me that when she joined there were about 30 members in the North Wales Association and meetings were held in the Talardy Hotel, St Asaph or in Llandudno. One or two meetings were held in the University College of Wales, Bangor, through the Secretary's husband – Professor Bleddyn Roberts. Members attended from a wide area and meetings were held quarterly.

Catrin became President of the MWF in 1973-74, the first time a Welsh woman had held this office and in that year the Council came to Swansea for one meeting and to North Wales to Prestatyn for the other. She invited Dr William Evans, the eminent Cardiologist, to be the guest speaker in Swansea. He had retired to live in his birthplace, Tregaron, in 1967 after 40 years in the London Hospital. When Council came to North Wales I remember that they were entertained to a Medieval Banquet in Ruthin Castle with Dr Nerys Evans' husband, Dr Glyn Evans as the memorable Baron. Catrin chaired the proceedings in a cool, calm and collected way – as always unflappable. Dr Nerys Evans was our North Wales Representative on Council and spoke at the meeting. I remember many delegates saying that they had been impressed at the way Catrin had handled the proceedings with good humour.

She was Careers Advisor for Medical Women for North Wales from 1969 until after she retired and helped many women to complete their training and advised them on their career prospects. It was due to MWF pressure that the retainer and retraining schemes were initiated and in North Wales we were fortunate to reap the benefit of these schemes.

She attended her first meeting of the Medical Women's International Association (MWIA) in Baden-Baden, Germany following which she regularly attended all their meetings – in the Philippines, Japan, Australia, Guatemala, Canada and Berlin.

She became Procedure Adviser to the MWIA and was North European Vice-President 1992-1995 and in 1995 she became an Honorary Member of the MWIA. She thought that the achievements of the MWF was greater 40 years earlier when the retainer and retraining schemes were introduced. Now MWF is consulted on Green Papers (1996) and there is a regular meeting with the Junior Minister of Health. The MWF is more GP orientated than previously and Consultants are not so interested.

With the MWIA, matters applying to one country may not be applicable in others. They are of more help to developing countries as they can quote advice received from the MWIA to support their cause. When she was Vice-President she visited all the countries of Northern Europe. She found standards in Latvia terrible as they had no money and women had to pay for family planning. In Russia there was no family planning and women could have up to 25 abortions. Women were Assistant Professors but did not become Heads of Departments. In Lithuania there was a hatred of Russia because they couldn't get Russian Citizenship. She met the first Russian Astronaut, Valentina Terashkova who told her that her daughter was a Doctor and she had been told she would never get to the top because she was a woman. Catrin felt we were going the same way with the percentage of women Consultants going down and the percentage of women in Sub-Consultant grades going up. [This was in 1996].

She went to China twice and found it quite primitive, although Shanghai was the first place where microsurgery was started. She saw a Sarcoma being removed from the mid-humerus and the arm sutured back. Acupuncture works well there and it takes three years of training to practice it. In Beijing they are going back to natural medicine. Barefoot Doctors were equivalent to Health Visitors and here would be Nurses. She attended the second United Nations Congress – the Decade of Women, in Nairobi, Kenya in 1985 and the Third Congress in Beijing in 1995. At the Non-Governmental Organisations (NGO) Forum in Nairobi she represented the Wales Assembly of Women and at the Government Conference she was one of the MWIA Observers.

In Beijing they got more out of the Governmental than Non-Governmental organisation meetings which were held one hour's drive outside the city. There was violent opposition to the Congress as the Government did not want 30,000 women who spoke their mind in the city. During the first week of their visit the Chinese women spoke to them but by the second week they didn't do so because of the presence of video cameras. It was impossible for delegates to go to everything as there were so many meetings. The MWIA ran one meeting in the NGO Forum and the World Health Organisation (WHO) took the Governmental part of the meeting; both interesting. MWIA is an affiliated Body to the NGO and report to the WHO and regional conference of the United Nations, so they have official status with the United Nations.

The Northern European Association was the first to hold regional conferences and she has attended them in Denmark and Brighton. The first time in 1995 was in Lubeck and America held its first in 1995 also. Denmark and Finland have recruited Members and Norway was being resurrected. In Holland there were increasing numbers of Lesbians and an interest in Euthanasia.

As Procedures Adviser to the MWIA she advised the Chairman on Resolutions and whether they were in order, and would go through everything beforehand with the President so that they had a united front.

In 1978 the Shah of Persia was deposed and the 1980 proposed Conference of the MWIA in Persia cancelled. At short notice, the Conference was relocated to Britain, in Birmingham, and Catrin became the Chair of the Organising Committee. Between 700-800 medical women from all over the world attended and Catrin was very busy as well as being a carer for her mother. Dorothy Ward became a great friend and helper at this time. She had met Catrin when the MWF visited Rhyl in 1974 and they met regularly at Council meetings. She regarded Catrin as a role model and a mentor, who she turned to for advice when she became Chairman of MWF and MWIA. Dorothy thought her a clear thinker of common sense who could unravel woolly thoughts. Catrin was skilful in getting motions through committees and did not offend others in doing so. She was a good listener and would give her opinion in a few succinct words. "Well, lets be quite honest" was another memorable phrase to make one think.

The Birmingham Conference was a great success and was opened by the Duchess of Gloucester who afterwards agreed to become Patron of MWF. My husband Elwyn would take any money collected during the conference to the Bank night safe for safe-keeping overnight so that they did not have to keep it in their rooms.

She felt that the MWF does not have a good system now as there is one Council meeting with the AGM and it is rubber stamping. The Executive Committee meets once a quarter and takes the decisions. There is no standing Committee other than Ethics, which is an Advisory Group. There is no grass roots opinion and it is run by London. At the time of the interview (1996) there was no Welsh Member on the Executive of the MWF. She thought the Federation was going down hill with a lack of enthusiasm as women don't realise its value. She certainly felt it had lost its way and became disillusioned with it. At the present time (2010) Olwen Williams, Consultant Physician in Sexually Transmitted Disease, has been elected on to the Executive.

Catrin was the MWF Representative on the Women's National Commission for 11 years being elected three times. She was grateful to Professor David Jones, CAMO and Clwyd Health Authority for allowing her to attend the meetings of the Women's National Commission. She was elected Co-Chairman for two years (1981-1983) with Lady Janet Young as Chairman. They looked at all the White Papers and made sure that the views of women were made known. It was one of two Advisory Bodies to the Cabinet and was serviced by the Cabinet Office, now the Department of Employment. The original Government Co-Chairmen were Mrs Barbara Castle, Mrs Margaret Thatcher and Lady Janet Young. She thought Mrs Castle and Mrs Thatcher used the same Hairdresser as their hair dye was the same colour. They were similar in character, but their style of politics was different. Mrs Thatcher was an excellent Chairman but after her appointment, pulled up the ladder after her. She was afraid of women and surrounded herself with "yes" men.

When Barbara Castle was running down Consultants, Catrin told her that provincial Consultants worked very hard teaching their junior staff. Janet Young was Leader of the House of Lords at the time and Margaret Thatcher sacked her. Catrin had made an innocent remark at a Downing Street party to Mrs Thatcher and she thought that this was what had led to the sacking.

Catrin as Co-Chairman (1981-1983) took over when the Chair wasn't present and she worked hard to keep up to date. Meetings were held once a quarter and she attended Working Groups. As Chair she was on all Groups Ex-officio – Law Reform, Green Papers, International Sub-Committees, Reform of Prostitution Laws, Abortion, Abuse, Children in Hospital, etc.

She was past Chairman of East Denbigh and Flintshire division of the BMA, a Member of the Welsh Council and North Clwyd Representative to the Annual Representative Meeting. At one time she was a Member of the Court of the University College of North Wales, Bangor and Member of the General Advisory Committee of the BBC for 4-5 years representing North Wales.

She has been a Founder Member, becoming Vice-President in 1984 and past Executive Committee Member of the Wales Assembly of Women. She was also a Founder Member and Chairman of Wales Women's European Network. She sat on the UN Women's Advisory Committee as a MWF Representative. She was a Welsh Representative of the Women's European Lobby. She was the MWF Member of an Ad-Hoc Working Group chaired by Dame Ann Speakman who reported on "Women and the NHS!". She gave talks on radio and television advising the public on problems of coping with Cancer and Laryngectomy.

She gave unstintingly of her time, talent and energy to her patients and the causes she supported. She supported women and medical women in particular. An unassuming woman of integrity, caring, energetic and optimistic whose glass was always half-full. She wasn't interested in worldly things, nor was she a socialite. Money and trappings meant nothing to her and she didn't flaunt her achievements. She could be reserved and secretive and I would glean things piecemeal when she was prepared to tell me something. She was a tireless, meticulous worker whose life was full of interest, who inspired loyalty and high standards and was discrete. Manners were also important.

She didn't marry or have children, but she had charm, was quick witted, had a repartee and humour and had friends in all walks of life. Her childhood sweetheart joined the RAF and was killed, and although she enjoyed men's company she was never one of the boys. In fact, she was quite a lady who enjoyed her home and garden.

After her father died, her mother came to live with her and she cared for her until her death at the time of Catrin's retirement (1986). On Catrin's trips abroad she would ring home regularly to make sure all was well with her mother. Before Catrin went into a Nursing Home in Rhyl, she was well cared for by two men – Ray and John and their wives and they remained helping her to the end.

Catrin had a full life. Her greatest loss I'm sure was the loss of her brother, but I don't think she would have changed her life in any way. Ethics were important to her and so was compassion for people. In retirement she thought one should have plenty of interests. She gave the Dame Hilda Rose Lecture when the MWF Council visited Llandudno in 1996 and in it pointed out that the Equal Opportunities Commission is not for positive discrimination for women but was for equality of opportunity for women. She reminisced about her life and philosophies. She told us she was very much desired as a child and indulged to a certain extent but there was a thin red line that she wasn't allowed to cross. She talked about the medical advances in her lifetime – Cochlea Implants, the problem caused by ageism and the problem for women in undeveloped countries. If she was alive and I was to ask her today what life has taught her I'm sure she would say – there's more to be done – keep at it.

Retirement isn't a word one associates with Catrin for she continued to interest herself in voluntary causes to do with her speciality and Disability Wales and became a Trustee of the North Wales Resources Centre in Ysbyty Glan Clwyd, re-named Ty Nerys for a short time but this title was removed by the Betsi Cadwalader Health Board. It was largely through her influence that Disability Wales extended its interests to help those with sensory (hearing) impairment, as well as those with physical disability.

Catrin spent the last couple of years of her life in Preswylfa Nursing Home, Rhyl and would be taken back to her home by Ray for visits. Her friends visited her regularly and she was well looked after. She continued to attend Disability Wales meetings with Nerys Hughes and during the Spring before she died went to a meeting in Cologne. Fortunately, her mind was clear until her last illness when she had a Stroke followed by Bronchopneumonia and returned to Glan Clwyd where she died quite quickly on 9th October 1998 aged 77. She was cremated in Colwyn Bay and on 13th February 1999 a service of thanksgiving for her life and work was held in Hebron Chapel, Old Colwyn. Miss Lilian Roberts her former Secretary and Mrs Lois Harrison, a Senior Nursing Officer gave solos.

Professor Robert Owen, a childhood family friend, read the lesson from Ecclesiastes and spoke of her as a dedicated and conscientious Surgeon who gave her best for her patients. Dr Narain, her Assistant, spoke on the ENT scene and Dr Bridie Wilson on the Welsh Woman's scene. David Livermore, Chairman of RNID spoke on her work for the deaf and Dr Dorothy Ward spoke on her involvement with the National and International Scene. There is much in her life worthy of recording for posterity, Bridie Wilson said in her Memorial Service. It is a pity that much of this has been lost.

Of all her achievements I think she would like to be remembered for her services to children. She enjoyed playing with children on the ward and mending their toys, getting on better with children alone but she would listen to the mothers of deaf children.

She would provide a whole range of services but was not afraid to say no and said "the wise Surgeon knows when to keep his hands in his pockets". Towards the end, the third generation of patients would attend her clinic. David Livermore described her as being a Key Trustee to the RNID – a wise woman of integrity who was modest and when she stood down as a Trustee the Board unanimously agreed to recognise her invaluable contribution.

Catrin was a friend for over 40 years and a Surgeon with whom I worked for 30 years. She led a very full, interesting life and achieved a great deal, planning the move of the ENT Department from St Asaph to the new District General Hospital in 1980. I think the death of her little brother spurred her on to pack as much as she could into her life. You could say, that her work was her life and I doubt that she had any regrets.

She was President of the local Save the Children Fund, the Royal British Legion and the Royal College of Nursing. A true internationalist who travelled the world and had friends in many countries. She has been an International Ambassador for Wales.

She was determined to keep going and could be domesticated: Narain was surprised to find her one day mending a hem of a skirt with a hand-held machine. Her father had a great influence on her life and was very proud of her achievements. She was also influenced by Mr Robert Owen, ENT Surgeon – Cardiff, who supported her and I think she would have liked to return to work in his Department. The last 6-7 years of her life were difficult, as she developed an acute demyelinating disease which was treated in Liverpool by Immunotherapy and she developed age-related macular degeneration, and became almost blind. She had started limping, then had to use a crutch and eventually a wheelchair. She had a lift installed in her home and when I told her she could get a grant – and "what would it cost?", she said "blow the cost – I'm having it". She wasn't prepared to wait, but unfortunately she wasn't able to use it a lot. She didn't like to have women in her home, but preferred to have men to help her.

After her death the ENT Department donated a chair in her memory with her name on it, and also the words 'the first ENT Surgeon in North Wales', to the Royal Society of Medicine Head Quarters in London. Narain was asked to go to the ceremony but declined and instead Mr Hammad attended to donate the chair.

Chapter Eight

June Pope Arnold MD, FRCP [1924 -]
First Consultant Geriatrician in North Clwyd [1961-1985]

Chance often plays a major turning point in life and this was certainly true for June Arnold in deciding to undertake a Medical Career and later in entering the new speciality of Geriatrics or Care of the Elderly as it is called now.

I had met her for a short time when we were both working in the Central Middlesex Hospital, London in the early 1950's and when I arrived in Rhyl she was a Medical Registrar working in her home town. I was invited to her home and made to feel very welcome by her parents who were delightful. They both contributed generously to the cultural life of the town and on a stone wall of the Town Hall is a plaque in memory of her mother. Her father was the first qualified Accountant in Rhyl.

On qualifying in 1948 she realised the limitations of her practical knowledge and that if she wished to travel to visit friends and work in Australia she would need further training. Her first year was spent in Liverpool where she did two jobs – six months Medicine and six months Surgery before going to work in Chase Farm

Hospital, London. This was as Senior Houseman with Dr Alan Birch, where she learnt to drink Pink Gin and improve her Bridge and took part in a hospital skit. Off duty was one weekend in six and a half day a week but with having to be back in the hospital by 10:00 pm to do a night round of her patients.

She did a Paediatric house job at the Central Middlesex Hospital, at the same time as Phyllis George, Desmond Julian, Margery Ashcroft and Chris Wood were also working there – all later making great contributions in Medicine.

She found Paediatric work very distressing because at the time very little could be done to help children who had dreadful deaths from Renal Failure and Leukaemia. The use of Antibiotics was beginning. She was involved in the early use of Streptomycin intrathecally for TB Meningitis and had success with this. She found telling parents that nothing could be done to save their children too stressful and decided to change course and become a General Practitioner. As preparation for this she did an Obstetric job with Mr O V Jones in St David's Hospital, Bangor for six months.

Then she decided the time had come to visit Australia for six months not as an Emigrant paying £10 but paying full fare, on board the "Morton Bay" of Shaw Savill Line. There was a six week voyage out – the ship was damaged in Malta but managed to get to Freemantle. From there she travelled by train to Perth then to visit "Bull Finch Goldmine" by overland train and on to Adelaide. There was one other English girl on the train travelling first class on her own and she had the use of the Observation Car. June was upgraded and able to travel with her so that they both had congenial company and she found to her amazement that the girl's sister was a Senior Registrar in Obstetrics in Wrexham, whom she knew.

She stayed in Adelaide for some time before going on to work in Penola in South Australia which was halfway between Adelaide and Melbourne. Here she worked for three weeks as a General Practitioner. This was a very wooded area full of Greeks and Italians who were not bothering to learn the English Language as they were there to make money to send home before returning to their families. They worked in the Saw Mills where they purposely frightened her by putting their hands too close to the saws.

Life was primitive, the General Practitioner's house had holes in the roof and the lavatory was in the garden, as was the custom everywhere at the time. The Principal and his wife had two children then, eventually having six. The days were long and hard and she hardly had time to see them. Operations started at 7:00 am, he doing the surgery and she giving the anaesthetic. Ethyl Chloride followed by Ether on an open mask she preferred to using the home made anaesthetic machine which was either all on or off. The men who were burly, took a lot of anaesthetic which was impossible to regulate, and they needed restraining to keep them on the operating table.

After two hours, morning surgery followed with all patients taking 15 minutes with no question of hurrying the consultation as they paid. It was winter, seemed to rain all the time, was very cold and she needed an electric fire to keep her feet warm. She had a small Austin A30 car without windscreen wipers and for visits to outlying surgeries there were no roads but she had to negotiate by compass and directions on how to get to her destination. Fortunately, she did not get lost although she was alone. On one visit she saw a man who had a huge log fall across his pelvis and as she had no X-Ray facilities sent him to Adelaide. After a few days he returned as no fracture was shown. Another man had a displaced cartilage which she could not reduce and she sent him to Melbourne. She felt her standing was reduced by these incidences and the men did not come to her clinics.

The day was taken up by surgeries and visits, and between 10:00 pm and 11:00 pm she met the Principal to work out the financial business of the Practice.

After Penola she went to Melbourne and then to the Barrier Reef. She saw "Sugar Parties", which were parties held to celebrate the awarding of Contracts for sugar on large estates, and became aware of the Quota System for Sugar. Then to Sydney and on to New Zealand before returning home as a Ship's Doctor on the "Melbourne Star" which was a ship of the Blue Star Line (Vesty's). This was a new cargo ship as the Merchant Navy was depleted during the War and many new ships were built afterwards. Not many cargo ships carried any Doctors, those that did were liable to be called to other ships in the Pacific. As the only Doctor on board she would be expected to carry out surgery and on looking up the Procedure Book on board for Appendicitis was given the advice – steer for the nearest port. As she was in the middle of the Ocean this was not much use but fortunately she was not called to do this.

Her worst problem was Psychiatric on the way home. Two friends who had not met for 20 years planned to take a holiday in Britain and one of them became deranged on the boat. She tried various drugs and referred her to see a Consultant Psychiatrist in Harley Street as soon as they arrived.

When the ship passed Dover Castle a salute was made to Lord Vesty whose home it was and when they arrived in the Thames they had to wait 12 hours for the tide to be right to berth in Albert Dock. A frustrating time as they could hear people talking on land yet they could not leave the ship. They had picked up oil in Caracas because of the 1956 Suez Crisis and the ship was so heavy that it bumped the bottom on berthing at sunset.

When she arrived back in Rhyl intending to join a General Practice she discovered that her father had met by chance one of the local Consultant Physicians who had advised him that General Medicine and General Practice were over subscribed. He suggested that she should train in the new speciality of Geriatrics where there would be many openings including a local one. At this time she had a broad training which included several medical posts; Surgery, Obstetrics, Paediatrics and General Practice – as well as a brief spell in Australia and experience as a Ship's Doctor. She decided to follow the advice given and spent two years working with the pioneer, Dr Marjorie Warren, at the West Middlesex Hospital and then as a Senior Registrar at Whittington Hospital with Dr Exton-Smith.

From Dr Warren she learnt about the importance of rehabilitation and with Dr Exton-Smith was involved in several research projects which included the Value of Hospital Treatment in the Elderly and the Domiciliary Assessment of Social Problems.

Dr Exton-Smith was very keen on gadgets and believed in working as a team with Nurses and Therapists. He helped to develop the Zimmer Frame which converted a ward of chair-bound patients into ambulant ones. They showed that if patients were admitted at the start of their illness very few were still in hospital after three months. At that time elderly people with disabling diseases were very reluctant to enter hospital until their relatives could no longer cope.

In the early sixties Geriatric Departments for the active treatment and rehabilitation of the elderly sick were being developed throughout the country, but when she became a Senior Registrar there were only four such posts - at Sunderland, Oxford, Scotland and the Whittington Hospital in London. The aim of the Departments was to successfully treat illness. As degenerative disease was so common, complete cure was unusual and many patients had several disorders at the same time. They also aimed to improve the patients' ability to look after themselves and place them in surroundings suited to their capabilities and continued well-being. This work was coordinated with the domiciliary and welfare services available to the elderly in the community.

Whilst she was at Whittington Hospital she carried out with Dr Exton-Smith the Domiciliary Assessment of Social Problems in the Elderly using a practical scoring system, which was found to be a valuable tool for judging their needs for nursing and personal assistance and also the extent to which this would cause a burden to their Carers. By collaboration with General Practitioners and Social

Workers they found they were able to avoid hospital admission in one third of those referred to hospital on social grounds. Sixty percent of patients admitted to hospital were able to return to their own home after rehabilitation and were less of a burden to their relatives. Another paper at that time showed the value of hospital treatment for the elderly.

June was appointed Consultant Geriatrician by the Welsh Hospital Board in 1961 to provide a service for the elderly for the Clwyd and Deeside Group of Hospitals. When she took up her appointment there were two Physicians in post in Rhyl – Dr D E Meredith and Dr G H T Lloyd and they both made her welcome from the start and were helpful to her, making life easy. She was included in the Consultant On-Call Rota for emergencies working one in three or one in two when one was away so she had a foothold in the Royal Alexandra Hospital which was the base hospital. Her beds were in HM Stanley Hospital, St Asaph and Lluesty Hospital, Holywell; both old workhouses with dormitory provision for able-bodied people reached by awkward stone staircases. In Lluesty there were two wards provided by a lift as well. She had a total of 194 beds, 149 at Lluesty and 45 at St Asaph. This was little over 1 bed per 1000 population not far off the suggested 1.2 beds per 1000. Most of the elderly population lived on the coastal belt, many in isolation as their partner had died and they had not made friends. She was able to cope with the majority of requests for admission as her waiting list in 1964 was rarely more than 12 and waiting time rarely more than a month. In addition, she used convalescent beds at St Clare's Convent Pantasaph to give people confidence that they could go home. She had decided on her policy before starting the job and stuck by it feeling she had to resist outside pressure.

One wing of the cross of 45 beds in the old workhouse in St Asaph was empty and decorated when she arrived which was a great help and she found good support given by the Pathologists for post-mortem examinations and blood investigations including a blood collecting service at Lluesty. Dr Tim Alban Lloyd was the first

Pathologist to the area and was very supportive, and Dr E V Pierce Williams was willing to provide Radiology facilities including Barium Meal and Enema investigations at first as was Dr Rodney Green afterwards.

Her Nursing Staff was excellent, but she admitted that life must have been very hard for Sister Minnie Williams who was very good, willing and prepared to alter to provide an up to date service for patients. In retrospect she felt she had been ruthless in her policy of putting up extra beds in order to keep her admission beds open.

As I said, she had written out her policy for the service before starting and the hub of this was her Secretarial Staff. She was greatly helped by Mrs Davies in St Asaph and by Mrs Lloyd in Lluesty. All the calls for admission were made to Mrs Davies and everybody was admitted whom the General Practitioner thought was urgent. Lluesty admitted patients for rehabilitation and for long stay care. Bed space between beds was increased so that patients learnt to cope as her philosophy was to get people home and to convince them that they could cope. St Clare's Convent was a halfway house where people learnt they could dress themselves and walk to the lounge or dining room. This catered for between 10 and 60 patients with the average being 30.

Dr Alban Jones, Chief Administrative Medical Officer for North Wales, negotiated the facility and the Convent was to be reimbursed £8 per week per head. Before her arrival Lluesty was regarded as a place where patients did not get up and were left to die. She had to prove to them that they could do things and encouraged them to get better. Sister Immaculata was dedicated to assisting the patients who came to her, the General Practitioner did regular ward rounds and June did a weekly ward round to assess progress.

June also had to overcome problems with relatives who felt they could not cope and organised a scheme for patients to be admitted for six weeks followed by being at home for six weeks - the first respite care system in Wales. The Right Honourable Richard Crossman M.P. as Secretary of State for Health set up a committee to look at Geriatric and Psychiatric services which was chaired by Dr Gwilym Hooson, a General Practitioner from Holywell and a member of the Welsh Hospital Board who was one of June's Clinical Assistants so she had a direct line of influence on this. This was helpful, and money came when the District General Hospital was built to provide acute geriatric beds in Glan Clwyd; a Psycho-geriatric Unit at the North Wales Hospital for Nervous Diseases, Denbigh and a Rehabilitation Unit for Lluesty as well as a Day Hospital.

She developed a good relationship with General Practitioners and made home visits out of hours. Gwilym Hooson would collect 2-3 patients for her to assess on the same visit and the General Practitioners were also helpful in convincing the lay public that the service was a good one as they were not keen at first. Lluesty remained a problem because it had been a Workhouse, and because of its location – it was too far for visitors and had poor public transport arrangements, although the Rotary Clubs were helpful in providing car lifts for relatives.

Dr G W Roberts, the Chief Administrative Medical Officer for Clwyd had progressive ideas on Homes for the Elderly and they were well run with a Nurse in Charge and Night Staff so it became easier to send frailer people there. Patients could have their own General Practitioner in these, but one GP was in charge adminis-tratively. New Homes were built in most towns and June was involved in their design which included providing lifts.

Another innovation was the creation of a ward at Lluesty for elderly Orthopaedic patients to be rehabilitated following trauma or major Orthopaedic surgery. This was in collaboration with Mr Robert Owen, Orthopaedic Surgeon who later became Professor of Orthopaedic Surgery in Liverpool. Patients were admitted to the ward within 20 minutes of a phone call in an emergency.

She had no help when she first arrived in the area then had a Senior Hospital Medical Officer in St Asaph, a General Practitioner, Dr Geoff Robinson. In the mid 1960's she had a Registrar, the first being Dr Izzat. Twenty four hour cover by General Practitioners was provided at Lluesty by Drs G Hooson, D Williams, Joseph, J Barnard, J Curley, Parry and G O Jones. It was a fight to get money to pay them.

She later became part of the Registrar Rotational Scheme and had a new Registrar every six months. When the second Geriatrician was appointed, this appointment was shared so she only had a Registrar for half a year. It was also difficult to get central money for the second Geriatrician post and Dr B Bhowmick was appointed as a Locum Consultant at first. At this time she became a member of several committees in order to make her case for extra posts. She was able to negotiate a Senior Registrar by arranging a scheme whereby the person would spend one day a week with Professor John Brockenhurst, Manchester who was a friend of hers.

When the second Consultant was appointed her Secretary left at the same time and two new Secretaries were appointed, one each; her idea of having a central admission point was not seen as necessary by her colleague who had not done Geriatrics in any other unit. The Department now has six Consultants who all get on together and it is a University Department with a Senior Lecturer. She feels sorry that during her later years as a Consultant her ideas of sharing did not come off but she is glad that the Department she created is so successful, and that it is part of the Department of the Care of the Elderly of the Welsh School of Medicine.

She had been involved in several initiatives. Carrying out Assessment of Geriatric Units for the Health Advisory Department gave her lots of ideas. She, as a Consultant, was the Chairman of the Team which included two Nurses, an Administrator and a Therapist. The Right Honourable David Ennals M.P., Secretary of State for Health came to chat to them and they obtained special finance to carry out their work. Each assessment took six weeks and visits were made to Cornwall, Wiltshire and NW Thames. In the early days of the Hospital Advisory Service the Team was sometimes able to persuade the Secretary of State to make a special allocation to implement their recommendations. She received a lot of help from Dr Eluned Woodford-Williams, a Consultant Geriatrician in Sunderland and the Director of the Hospital Advisory Service, who told her before the second Consultant was appointed that her Department was of a high standing in the Country, the rest being in the big cities. She got a lot of interesting commitments through her.

She was asked to be a Consultant Assessor for 4-5 Geriatric complaints and was involved in assessing Senior Registrar training posts. It was difficult for her to be away too much whilst she was involved in acute work but she attended many committees and enjoyed playing a part in Post Graduate Training. She went to Cardiff to sit on the Geriatric Sub-Committee of the Welsh Medical Committee, the Welsh Postgraduate Committee and Senior Registrar Committee. She became Secretary of the Royal College of Physicians, Senior Registrar Training Committee for seven years and was a member of the Council and Executive Committee of the British Geriatric Society. Her great contribution was recognised in 1995 by the Award of a Medal of the British Geriatric Society.

Since her retirement in 1985 she has had no involvement in Medical Committees which she missed as well as the companionship of working closely with other Doctors and Nurses. She was, however, involved for several years in assisting Senior Nurses from the Royal College of Nurses, in selecting Nurses for British Geriatric Society Scholarships. She also served as the British Geriatric Society Representative on the pre-retirement Council. Despite this she is derogatory about her achievements. She regrets that because of lack of resources she was unable to manage her service less rigidly. It was very hard for patients to be cared for so far from home and she was never able to overcome the aversion to Lluesty despite the excellent care provided. Because of the enormous number of patients she saw and helped back to a useful life she was unable to remember them all if she met them outside the hospital and feels let down by this.

Looking back over 50 years of the NHS she thinks it was a wonderful idea and the envy of the World. She regards the constant reorganisation since 1974 as bad and feels it should have stayed under Hospital Management Committees as she did not like the District Management Team and would have preferred a Medical Superintendent who did not have beds. She thinks the small team in place now is better, although admits she is not working with it.

She likes the way that junior appointments are now linked and it is not so important to move around for jobs and may be having periods where one was not working which would affect pension rights. She was used to working as part of a team in Geriatrics early on and now more people are seeing the advantage of this and it is getting widely adopted. The recruitment of Therapists who are so important in rehabilitation is also becoming easier, facilities are better and there are more of them.

She is interested in the way that the NHS specialist service developed from nothing in 1948 and now each district has specialists of high standard. Many Doctors who came to work in Rhyl had distinguished careers and helped to launch their respective specialities.

June, the eldest of three daughters, had been born in Rhyl on the 9th February 1924. She attended a private school in Pendyffryn Road, Rhyl which became known as The Poplars, passing the Entrance examination to the County School, which later became Rhyl High School.

She had been interested in Natural Sciences but decided, with her father's encouragement, to study Medicine and went to Leicester University College to study for the Intermediate Examination in Botany, Zoology, Chemistry and Physics before proceeding to Liverpool University where she enjoyed her training in Medicine.

During her career she had been Chairman of Rhyl Music Club, Rhyl Arthritis Club (ARC) and Rhyl Save the Children.

After retirement she became Chairman of the Friends of Bodelwyddan Castle and later a Trustee. Over the summer she is a

108

Welcomer in St Asaph Cathedral and at one time helped with a Luncheon Club for lonely people, which later discontinued.

Unfortunately she developed arthritis after retirement but that has not prevented her from being a great traveller. She remains interested in Archaeology, the History of Medicine, Save the Children and her local Church in Tremeirchion.

June felt that Dr David Meredith, Dr Marjorie Warren and Dr Exton Smith influenced her life in pursuing a career in Geriatrics. She started working at the time the NHS started, when Doctors were unused to the service they were to provide and pushed themselves to the limit work wise. Although they were entitled to two weeks holiday every six months, she was told that it would be unwise to ask for it in her first job. She didn't think there was a glass ceiling for women in Medicine but there could be in other fields. She would have liked to have lived differently with more time for hobbies, leisure, sport and to develop further interests; but the long hours worked in Medicine were not conducive for this when the NHS started. This has now changed.

Chapter Nine

Muriel Margaret McLean MD, FRCP, DCH [1920-1991]
Consultant Paediatrician, Rhyl (1957-1980)
(Great, Great, Great Granddaughter of Robert Burns
– on her mother's side)

Muriel McLean's arrival in Rhyl caused quite a stir in Medical circles as we, who were already working there, were expecting a man who was known to be the favourite to be appointed. A better choice could not have been made. We knew she must have been very good, as the only woman against the men short listed for the post and we were not disappointed. Possessed of a fine intellect and enquiring mind, she set up and ran a Paediatric Service as the sole Consultant in Paediatrics until some three years before her retirement.

In 1955 Muriel McLean, her mother, and others of her family spent a holiday in Llanfairfechan and when the first full time Consultant Paediatric appointment was advertised for Rhyl shortly afterwards she discussed with her Professor, whether she should apply. She was told she had no chance but the experience would be good practice. However, she gained the appointment and the preferred male candidate was not too pleased! She had enjoyed the family holiday and chance brought her back to Wales, where she remained for the rest of her life. Her mother joined her in her home in Prestatyn, for around that time her family had dispersed from Scotland and there was no reason for her to stay there. Now the family base was with Muriel and it was here that Vida, her sister, came to live when she retired from her teaching career which had taken her to the Orkneys, Nigeria, Liverpool and Banchory in Scotland. She arrived in Prestatyn a year before her mother died in 1977, and consequently Muriel was fortunate to have the companionship of her family, practically throughout her life.

Her post entailed being responsible for the care of sick children in the Children's Ward in the Royal Alexandra Hospital, Rhyl; a Unit of 18 acute medical beds and cots and also the care of the newborn in the Obstetric Unit having 54 cots in HM Stanley Hospital, St Asaph seven miles away which was very demanding. She held clinics and provided cover when needed in other hospitals in the area, including Llangwyfan where as a Scot she would have been particularly welcomed by Dr Biagi and his wife, and attended their hospital parties.

Anne Sutherland was a student in Aberdeen when Muriel was a Registrar and Anne joined her in Rhyl in 1963 where they worked well together until her retirement.

When she first arrived in Rhyl she shared a Houseman with Dr G H T Lloyd who had beds on the same floor and was a General Physician with an interest in Neurology. She had to cope with emergencies at night and would return home in the morning for a shower and breakfast before returning to work. Until Anne Sutherland joined her, Dr Gerald Roberts of Wrexham would cover her work when she took a holiday. She was firm with Ivor Lewis who wanted to keep children who had surgery on the Surgical Ward, and insisted that they be nursed on the Children's Ward. She was completely dedicated to the children who were under her care and provided a first class service under very trying conditions. Towards the end she had health problems but on retirement joined the Citizens Advice Bureau in Prestatyn, becoming its Chairman.

She was glad to retire in 1980 after seeing the Department move to Ysbyty Glan Clwyd. The last few years had been difficult with an increased workload, a new colleague with new ideas, and insufficient staff.

She had written a paper about the incidence of infantile pyloric stenosis in the North-East of Scotland, showing that the incidence had increased during the 16 years from 1938-1953. It was unlikely to have been a natural increase of the disease, but more probably due to more frequent diagnosis by the General Practitioner with increased tendency on his part to refer to Hospital any infant with persistent vomiting. She described an infant with auricular flutter which was diagnosed two days before delivery. Treatment with high dosage of digitalis resulted in normal cardiac rhythm in a month. She also reported a case of Chronic Idiopathic Hyper-parathyroidism associated with moniliasis. In 1966 she published in collaboration with Dr Charles Hilton Jones and Dr Anne Sutherland a report of an outbreak of Haemolytic – Uraemic Syndrome in North Wales.

The daughter of The Manse, Muriel was the fourth of five children of the Reverend David W McLean, a Minister in the Presbyterian Church of Scotland, and his wife who was the Great, Great Granddaughter of Robert Burns. Muriel was born on 26th May 1920 in the Parish of Gamrie, 8 miles from Banff. The eldest two children were twins Vida and Irene. A brother next called Ian who was eighteen months younger than the twins and who died before their mother. Another brother, David, who was four years younger than Muriel, became a Dental Surgeon of Hale near Manchester. Her family at first did not want to be associated with Robert Burns, but her father proposed the toast "the immortal memory" every year. He was proud of him as was David. David wasn't sure about Muriel but Vida didn't want to have anything to do with it.

Her father died in 1932 after a short illness from Pneumonia, when Muriel was 12 years old, and her mother was left with the five children and had to leave their tied home and moved to a bungalow in Banff. She was a very good manager financially and the children all did well. Muriel went to Banff Academy where she was always top of her class before proceeding to Aberdeen where she qualified in Medicine in 1942. This was a profession she had always wanted to follow.

Muriel worked in the Sick Children's Hospital in Glasgow and had a short period as a General Practitioner before joining the Royal Army Medical Core (RAMC) in 1944. She was posted to India and spent time at Rawalpindi and Abbottabad now in Pakistan, which she enjoyed very much and had a good time. She was discharged from the RAMC in 1947 and returned to Aberdeen. In her early years she had talked of being a Medical Missionary but later changed to Paediatrics. She worked as Paediatric Registrar and Senior Registrar at the Royal Aberdeen Hospital for Sick Children. In the Aberdeen Students Magazine the quote under her photograph was "she wants some red cells for a blue baby". This was a period when she attained her postgraduate qualifications – Diploma in Child Health in 1948, Membership of the Royal College of Physicians of Edinburgh in 1951 (elevated to Fellow of the College in 1959) and MD Aberdeen in 1955.

Muriel lived in Prestatyn in a well appointed detached house which had a large garden. She was a keen gardener and loved her dog which she enjoyed walking daily. As a student she had enjoyed walking and climbing in the Cairngorms. She used to enjoy tennis as a girl, had been a Girl Guide and played hockey as well. She didn't keep a diary and didn't write much, but was a great reader and loved playing Bridge in which she had always been interested and was skilful at it. At one time she played regularly with colleagues and later had a ladies circle. She was also a good cook and could produce delicious meals.

She died suddenly on the 7th May 1991 shortly after having taken her dog for a walk.

She was completely dedicated to her work and was thrilled when she had an up and over door installed in her garage so that she could drive straight in by using remote control when she arrived home in the middle of the night. Something that I also wanted when we moved to our present home. Although now this is common practice it was unusual at the time she had it installed.

She had a very good intellect and when she became Chairman of the Hospital Medical Staff Committee I was the Secretary and found her easy, with a sense of humour and supportive. When I became a Member of the District Management Team I was able to support her also when she needed more staff for her Department. Many of our male Consultants were sexist and didn't realise the worth and contribution of women Doctors – they thought a woman's place was in the home. This attitude was prevalent in pre District General Hospital days in the early years of the NHS in North Clwyd.

Dorothy Anne Sutherland MBChB, DCH [1928-1991]
Registrar – Paediatrics [1963-1967]
Associate Specialist – Paediatrics [1967-1988]

Anne enjoyed her medical training in Aberdeen and qualified in 1950, MB ChB. She was chosen as a female medical student in the third year of her course for the Elizabeth Garrett Anderson Scholarship which entailed spending a month working in Copenhagen, Denmark where she attended lectures and ward rounds and found their English was very good.

Her first appointment after qualification was as House Surgeon to

Mr Andrew Logan, Consultant Thoracic Surgeon. This was a very tough job and she assisted him in the Operating Theatre with the first patient on which he carried out heart surgery. She then worked in Bangour Hospital as a House Surgeon doing modules of general surgery, plastic surgery, obstetrics and gynaecology. Having never been to England, she marked a post advertised in the British Medical Journal and was appointed to Worthing as a House Physician before returning to Scotland to work in the City Hospital, Aberdeen. There she dealt with children who had Poliomyelitis and Typhoid. She then moved to Edinburgh as House Physician to the Royal Hospital for Sick Children before being appointed Registrar in Alder Hey Hospital to Dr Anne MacCandless. After that she worked as a Locum in General Practice where she was offered, but declined, a partnership before returning to Paediatrics.

At this time, Muriel McLean was trying to get a Registrar post in Paediatrics established in the Royal Alexandra Hospital, Rhyl and contacted Anne to ask her if she would like to join her in Rhyl as a Locum until this permanent post was approved. Anne was a student in Aberdeen when Muriel was there as a Registrar. She started in January 1963 as a Locum Registrar for three months at a salary of £25 per week, being told in the letter offering the Locum contract that there was no permanent appointment available at that time. This contract was renewed every three months at the same salary of £25 per week without any increase in increments, until 1965 when she had a letter saying that she had been short listed for the Registrar appointment. This was a standard letter from the Welsh Regional Hospital Board as it indicated she could visit the hospital if she wished to find out what the job entailed. At this time she had been doing the work for two years!

She was appointed and in November 1967 she was informed by letter that she had been successful in gaining a Medical Assistant appointment for two years in the first instance. This was made a permanent appointment in 1969. She was also able to purchase added years to her pension.

She and Muriel worked well as a team, along with excellent nursing staff in Rhyl and St Asaph. When Muriel went on holiday she acted as a Locum Consultant from 1971 onwards. They did all the Paediatrics for North Clwyd, the Unit having 18 acute medical cots and beds in Rhyl, and 54 cots in the Obstetric Unit in St Asaph which was seven miles away. This could cause very tricky situations if they were called urgently from one hospital to the other. Outlying hospitals were also covered in Colwyn Bay and in the Isolation Hospital, Bron-y-Nant. Traffic problems on the A55 between Abergele and Colwyn Bay necessitated getting there through inland villages in the days before the motorway was built. All problems were not solved until after Glan Clwyd Hospital opened, but even then despite the shorter distance to St Asaph, summer traffic could cause delays and problems. It had been pointed out to Clwyd Health Authority that there was potential for disaster if the Obstetric Unit was not moved to Glan Clwyd and it took a serious problem one weekend for them to act and transfer this Unit to the District General Hospital. It was officially opened by the Right Honourable John Redwood MP. Secretary of State for Wales in 1991.

Anne and Muriel provided a first class diagnostic clinical service. Special clinics were held once a month with Consultants from Liverpool attending. Mr Roger Cudmore, Paediatric Surgeon and Dr Wilkinson, Paediatric Cardiologist, provided excellent advice. Patients with problems were admitted to Alder Hey Hospital. It was all team work to give the children the best care and advice. Special Care of babies took up a lot of their time, as repeat exchange transfusion of the newborn required their constant attendance.

She, along with Muriel and Dr Charles Hilton-Jones Consultant Haematologist, published a paper in 1966 in Arch. Diseases of Childhood on Haemolytic Uraemic Syndrome which entailed considerable work in the monitoring and research into its cause.

Anne acted as a Medical Officer for the Cystic Fibrosis Trust from 1963 until she retired in 1988 and she also taught Midwives and Medical Students.

Anne has enjoyed her life and feels she was very lucky to come and work with Muriel. Although her job was time-consuming, she knew what it entailed and had excellent contact with nurses and other investigative departments.

She had bought her home Glan Faba in 1968 and when fellow Scot, Dr McLean's mother, came to have tea with her when her parents were staying, the conversation between them flowed. Anne came from a cultured, artistic Scottish background. Both her parents were Artists of the Edinburgh School – David Macbeth Sutherland and Dorothy Johnstone. Anne was born in Edinburgh on 2nd April 1928 as their second child, having one brother Iain who was nearly three years older than her. Iain entered the Foreign Office and had a long and distinguished career in the Diplomatic Service becoming Ambassador to Greece and ending as Ambassador to Moscow where he had started. Sadly, he died within a year of retirement.

She has enjoyed many foreign holidays with her sister-in-law, also with colleagues; June Arnold, Phillida Frost and Jean Green. She has enjoyed wildlife and RSPB holidays, remembering in particular a trip to the Galapagos Islands. She has had time to devote to painting and sketching and been to the South of France on a painting/wildlife holiday. She has attended many extramural classes on local history, archaeology, literature, art and drawing and taken many trips around these visiting Ireland and Swansea where she visited caves on the Gower Coast and a Gold Mine. She has been a member of the North Wales Wildlife Trust for many years and is past Chairman of the Denbighshire Branch.

She decided to study Medicine because she liked working with her head and her hands and Medicine, and in particular Paediatrics, has given her a fulfilled life. She played an important part in developing Paediatric services in North Clwyd, being held in great affection and respect. She undervalues her part in holding the service together and giving of her best with gentle humour and understanding of the needs of the sick child.

Chapter Ten

Jean Anne Green (née Evans) FRCS, DCH [1930 -]
Surgeon

Jean was a multi-talented child who could have been a professional Musician, a Scientist, Botanist or a Medical Woman. Her great-aunt, Dr Helen Wilson, was the first lady Doctor in Sheffield but gave it up to be a Christian Scientist. She took a great interest in Jean's career.

Jean was born in Sheffield on 25 May 1930 where her father, Reverend H O Evans BSc, was a Congregational Minister and an ardent Socialist, insisting that they lived in a terraced house in the slums amidst his poor working class congregation, which her mother hated. Jean was the middle of three children. Her sister Elizabeth (1928-2006), who was the eldest, read Botany in Glasgow and married a fellow Scientist who worked in the Nature Conservancy in Grange-Over-Sands. They emigrated to New Zealand where he worked in the New Zealand Forest Service, based in Rotorua and where they were very happy. Elizabeth died in 2006. Her brother, Oliver, was the youngest and he read Forestry in UCW Bangor and worked in the Ghana Forest Service. He died in 2004. Jean's mother, Gertrude Mary (Molly) was practical and could turn her hand to anything, her father was a great talker, and they were all keen walkers and cyclists.

When Jean was two years old they moved to Market Harborough where she started school and when she was eight they moved to Kendal until she was 18. She remembers her childhood as idyllic. She was sent to Milton Mount College in Sussex which was a school for Ministers' daughters, where she boarded. She enjoyed her time there and was happy, travelling to get there by train. She was not sporty as she was not good at running but she got into the school cricket team and became a wicket keeper. She also liked netball. She was in the Science stream in school and one of the choices for a career was Medicine. She hadn't thought of it beforehand but realised that it opened up the prospect of an interesting career. She was also interested in Botany and the natural world.

She started playing the Flute when she was 12 years old and has continued to do so throughout her life, playing in amateur orchestras, with groups and trios. In this casual way she has made a lot of friends. She also played the Oboe. Her mother had a friend who was an Oboist in the Hallé Orchestra and she gave her lessons about three times a year and in between she practised. She regretted not going to Music College, but her parents said she should do Medicine and after she qualified she could take a year off to study music. This never happened.

She applied to do Medicine in University College Hospital (UCH), London and had to undertake an intelligence test and interview before being accepted. UCH was one of the first places to use Intelligence Tests and she told me that she found it easy as she can see shapes and figures. She enjoyed UCH but found it lonely as it was a long way from home, but she had her Flute to play which was a help. She qualified in 1953 and did one year of house jobs there before moving to Liverpool, which she enjoyed and where she was within easy reach of her parents who had moved to Bangor.

Her first job in Liverpool was in Sefton General Hospital which was an eye-opener and her job was to prepare two wards of patients for surgery. It was a "culture shock" and the Consultant did ward rounds when she wasn't there. Before she started she had taken six months off to do a course for the Primary Examination of the Fellowship of the Royal College of Surgeons (FRCS) which she passed. After Sefton she did a Paediatric Casualty job in Myrtle Street Children's Hospital for six months, working with Isabella Forshall who was caring and exact, and where the atmosphere was completely different. Following that she worked in Alder Hey Hospital for two years and loved it. She had respect for Miss Isabella Forshall who told her "don't let their standards bring you down". She learnt how to talk to relatives and knew that she wanted to be a Paediatric Surgeon.

She moved to the Southern Hospital as a Junior Surgical Registrar in Casualty which was a responsible post, having a free hand from 9-5 and found the other Registrars helpful. It was here that she met Rodney and they got engaged to be married. He was a Senior Registrar and she a Junior Registrar when they got married, but she was a Fellow of the Royal College of Surgeons by this time (1957). Rodney was applying for a Consultant Post all over the place and was up against stiff competition as there were many applicants for each post. He'd heard that Rhyl was a good place medically, applied and was appointed. Jean was offered a job in Liverpool carrying out research in the Paediatric Department but she decided it would be impractical as she was pregnant. This was a 9-5 appointment which meant she would leave home at 7:30 am and not get back until almost 7:00 pm, driving both ways. She couldn't accept.

They moved to live in Tremeirchion, Denbighshire in a large family home with a garden outside the village. She and Rodney had four children. Jean was practical and enjoyed creating a lovely home and garden where she could cultivate the plants she wanted and where there was plenty of wildlife. They opened their garden at times to the public and enjoyed showing people around. All they did beforehand was mow the lawn and weed the flower beds. She continued to enjoy music and became Chairman of Denbigh Music

Club for a time. She had joined the club when they arrived; she plays in a group and was Second Oboe in the Philharmonia of North Wales. She also sings with the St Asaph Choral Society.

She joined the North Wales Wildlife Trust in the 1960's to help look after the countryside, purchase nature reserves and take groups of people around Y Graig – the Nature Reserve and Quarry outside Tremeirchion. This latter Reserve is very much her project which she has developed in a sensitive way with trails, bird boxes and notices for the public of what to look for. She managed Y Graig Reserve for 14 years. Jean has also published a book entitled "The Flowering Plants and Ferns of Denbighshire" in 2006. This is a checklist of Denbighshire plants at this time and the first time this has been carried out. It is a valuable record which will be useful for comparison when it is carried out in the future.

Jean was out of Medicine for ten years bringing up her children and enjoying domesticated family life. She was an excellent cook and they hosted parties in their home and raised money for charities. Her father died aged 58 years and her mother remained living in Bangor until she became incapacitated and moved to live with them. Jean returned to part time work in 1964 when she found a reliable home help.

She started working again during a Polio epidemic in the 1960's having been asked by Dr David Jones, Community Health Physician, to help him with the immunisation of hundreds of children in a mobile caravan which went to different towns. Her subsequent career in North Clwyd was varied. Rodney had asked Mr Ivor Lewis if there was work in his department and had been told "he'd never worked with a woman and wasn't going to start". This, despite his wife being his Anaesthetist!

She started in 1964 with two clinical assistant sessions for examining patients for ENT operations pre-operatively and then moved to examine newborn babies before they were discharged home. When Mr O M Jonathan arrived in the area she had work assisting him and going on ward rounds as part of his team, eventually undertaking the children's surgical operating lists and carrying on with this until he retired, doing two sessions per week.

In 1970 she started work in the Renal Unit working as part of Dr Keith Wright's team. This was new work and she went to the Transplant and Renal Unit in Liverpool for training. The Renal Unit, of which there were only two in Wales, was in the ground floor of Mercier House in Rhyl behind the Royal Alexandra Hospital. At first they were only able to treat one patient: when she left there were 50, and now 100 patients are having treatment in 2009. She was given study leave to go abroad to conferences in Prague, Budapest and Helsinki, and found these a boost to morale as everyone had the same problems which could be discussed. She had three sessions in the Unit for 16 years becoming an Associate Specialist and enjoyed it very much, working with a lovely team of nurses and a leader who was supportive of his Unit.

I met Mr Robert Sells, the retired Transplant Surgeon of Liverpool recently, who told me that there were never any problems with the fistula patients who came for transplants when Jean had carried out the surgery.

She got involved with Occupational Health in Hospital by accident, working first from H M Stanley Hospital before moving to premises in Glan Clwyd. She covered Glan Clwyd and H M Stanley Hospitals, and Dr Morton Evans covered Denbigh Infirmary and the North Wales Hospital.

Staff were screened before they started work by first completing a simple medical questionnaire which included details of past health and medication. If they were young and healthy, no further screening was necessary, but older staff were given a medical examination. She had a weight policy, in that anyone two stones over or under weight according to actuarial scale was only given a temporary contract for three months and advised what to do to correct their problem. The overweight had more absence from work because of sickness and she felt they had to have a policy and that everyone should have a medical. She wrote a pamphlet on how to avoid occupational problems at work.

She carried out environmental health surveys, accident and illness at work investigations, looked after resident sick Nurses and carried out immunisation and counselling. Her records showed 1307 consultations in 1979, 1439 in 1980 and 1578 in 1981. There was a high sickness rate due to the move to Glan Clwyd with 350 nursing days lost in June 1980.

She investigated occupational hazards and, for example, found the Telephonists worked in an overcrowded, dark, hot room with no fresh air and was able to get them moved to a better location in Glan Clwyd. She got air conditioning supplied to the Domestic Services Manager's office and CSSD. After working in this Department for five years she became redundant, possibly because of her strong views on obesity in staff.

She later undertook Colonoscopy Screening of patients and was given a Consultant Session to do this. Even though she wasn't able to pursue a straightforward surgical career she was able to use her skills and scientific training to carry out interesting and worthwhile work, which she enjoyed. She retired in 1986 when the Medical Defence Union raised insurance premiums and the Health Authority had a policy of not paying part-time Doctors' Medical Insurance or travelling expenses – not an inducement to get married women back to work!

In her retirement she has been involved in U3A in Abergele and every month in the summer takes groups for walks and talks about the wildlife in the area. It was a blow to her when Rodney died in 2002. He had had to give up driving his car and purchased an electric bike which he found too dangerous to ride around the country roads where they lived. He was a great character and as she said afterwards, "life was never dull with Rodney".

She feels she's had a happy life. She wanted to get married and knew when Rodney got a job in Rhyl that she would not achieve her ambition of being a Surgeon as surgery is demanding and there could be unexpected night emergencies. Rodney could not be expected to look after the children so it was a conscious decision not to proceed with her surgical career, as she couldn't cope with the unexpected. She liked working and liked the feeling of going out to work. Rodney encouraged her but expected her to be at home when he got back. When Rodney left the house he would tell her what needed to be done in the garden and she would reply "I'm going out".

If there are children in a marriage she feels they take priority and hers were dependent on her and she never neglected them. It depends on the spouse and circumstances if going back to work will be successful and it is important to sort things out beforehand and to have friends who would look after the children in an emergency. It also depended on the children, whether they accept a working mother. One of the children told her "Mari, poor thing, her mother is at home all day", a telling quote.

She did not think there was a glass ceiling for women. Women should be negotiators not fighters and wait until the time is right to get what they want. In the future, they need to take responsibility with diplomacy, not be wilting violets, be nice and "dress the part".

She is a proud mother and grandmother whose children have been a great boon for her. The eldest, Helen, is an IT Specialist in Mansfield College; Richard is a Motor Mechanic and lives in Gellifor, Sally is a General Practitioner in Oxford and has four children and Jeremy, the youngest, is a Radiologist and very much like Rodney - so Jean told me.

After Rodney died she decided to move out of their family home. She now lives in a smaller, compact property outside Denbigh where she has again created a tranquil garden and an area for wildlife, where she is happy pottering and which is in easy walking distance of the shops and buses. This is where she can continue to enjoy all her hobbies and friends.

Chapter Eleven

Gwyneth Parul Roberts MBE, BSc, MB BCh
'Pi Puii' – The Great One
[1st November 1910 – 29 January 2007]
Missionary – Anaesthetist – Community Worker

During the Service of Thanks-giving for her life in Rehobath Chapel, Prestatyn we were told by the Representative of the Church in India that when they heard of Gwyneth's death two thousand people in Durtlang attended the Service which had been held to mark their respect for and celebration of her memory. 'Pi Puii' – The Great One.

Gwyneth Parul Roberts had been a Missionary in Mizoram from 1938 to 1962, returning to look after her aged parents in Prestatyn and finding work as a Clinical Assistant in Anaesthesia and Trauma/Orthopaedics being well equipped to deal with both. She was the daughter of Missionaries but told me that she didn't have a calling to follow their footsteps, rather having followed an Aunt's advice to train to help women in Purdah in India who could not be seen by men other than their husbands.

She was an intrepid, fearless, strong-willed independent lady who supported wholeheartedly the causes she cared about. Mizoram and its people were certainly her first great love. She had been born on 1st November 1910 in Sylhet in Assam – now Bangladesh and christened Gwyneth Parul Roberts. Parul is a Bengali name meaning White Flower – "not at all a suitable name for me", she had told me years ago. It was a name of which she was proud and always signed Medical Registers as G Parul Roberts.

Her father, born in Liverpool of Welsh parents, had wanted to study Medicine but couldn't afford to do so. He obtained a Degree in Biology in the University College of North Wales (UCNW) Bangor and then read Theology in Aberystwyth and Bala. Her mother was born in Manchester and had trained as a Midwife and Teacher and in India became involved in helping girls. Her maternal grandfather had moved to Rhyl when his wife had become ill and after her death had been looked after by another daughter – Gwyneth's Aunt.

Gwyneth was their second child, the first having died and later a third child, a boy, was born. Gwyneth told me that he, Hywel, had a lovely temperament and he became a Consultant Surgeon in Newport. Gwyneth came to Wales first at the end of 1913, just three years old. When World War One (WWI) broke out her father returned to India and six months later her mother followed, leaving Gwyneth and Hywel in Wales. Gwyneth was brought up by her maternal Grandfather and her Aunt in Rhyl, whilst Hywel lived with an Uncle and Aunt in Croesor. They only saw each other during school holidays.

Her parents returned when she was 11 years old and when she was taken to London to meet them she felt very frightened as she didn't remember them. She went to Christchurch School, then the County School in Rhyl and then to UCNW Bangor to read Science as girls did not do this in Rhyl. She liked Biology but found Physics and Chemistry difficult, although she passed. She then proceeded to the Welsh National School of Medicine in Cardiff in 1928 and lived there with her mother and brother in a flat as her mother was home from India because of ill health.

Gwyneth was the only woman in her year for the first two preclinical years, and for self-protection she had her hair styled in an Eton Crop and wore a collar and tie so that she would not stand out from the men. When she started her clinical training two other girls joined her, but she told me that they were friends and she remained a 'loner'.

She enjoyed her student days and became involved in the Youth Movement of the Welsh Churches in Cardiff. She qualified in 1933 and after House jobs, she had further training in General Surgery, Gynaecology and Obstetrics in Cardiff, Wolverhampton and Manchester. She worked in Craig y Nos Hospital for some months to learn about Tuberculosis. She then studied at the London School of Tropical Medicine but following concussion failed the examination. She had received a good grounding in subjects which would be useful for her in India. As a daughter of Missionaries she had felt deprived of her parents as a child and told me that she and Hywel had been looked at as 'poor little children of Missionaries'. She had been forced to write to them but thought she had been well brought up by her Grandfather who she thought was more lenient with her, a headstrong child, than her father would have been.

She expected to be sent to Shillong but eventually was sent to Mizoram in 1938, which was the land of the enchanting Lushai Hills. This was one of the Districts of Assam until 1972 when it became Union Territory and on the 20th February 1987 it became the 23rd State of the Indian Union.

Mizoram is an area of strategic importance being flanked by Bangladesh in the West, Burma in the East and South, Assam and Manipur in the North. The temperature is pleasant, the Monsoon lasts from May to September, winter has some frost but no snow. Tropical forest clothed the steep and rugged hills. The Mizos are a Mongolian race and now 95% Christian. The economy is mainly

127

agriculture with some small scale industries being weaving, bamboo and cane.

When Gwyneth arrived in 1938 she was 27 years old and had travelled from Liverpool to Bombay by boat. Then she had a three week journey to get to Mizoram where she was to be the Medical Officer in charge of a Welsh Mission Hospital in Durtlang, in the North Mizo District of Assam, India. This was the only hospital where surgery was carried out for an area the size of Wales. When she arrived as the only Medical Officer, there was one other member of staff, the Matron, Miss Gwladys Evans. She had to adapt to a different culture and learn a new language. She was the first woman Doctor the Mizos had seen and no one before her had carried out surgery so she was very much a new phenomenon and it took two to three years for them to get used to her when many had to walk for days to get to the hospital. She found the Mizos full of fun and humour and liked them.

When she arrived Durtlang was a small village surrounded by jungle with common diseases being Malaria, Dysentery and Worms. The Hospital had been part of a Theological College and had a total of 40 beds in a male ward and a female ward including Maternity. There was a room for outpatients and another for an Operating Theatre and Labour Ward. The remaining beds were in another new similar building. The main problems when she arrived were the water supply, sanitation and the training of Nurses. It was just as well that she could turn her hand to anything for her first job was to build reservoirs to hold the water and to improve sanitation by building a septic tank. She taught the Mizos how to construct and use concrete. As there was no electricity for the first 20 years, surgery was carried out in daylight and if an emergency occurred at night, surgery was carried out using the light of paraffin lamps.

She slowly developed the Hospital to 120 beds and did everything including surgery, gynaecology and obstetrics. There was a great deal of peptic ulceration and she carried out gastrectomies. Tuberculosis was common and she carried out

Thoracoplasties under local analgesia. Most surgery was done under spinal anaesthesia, nerve blocks or local analgesia. Thyroidectomies were done under local analgesia and cervical block. If she had to use general anaesthesia she would induce with Ether or Chloroform on an open mask and then hand over to the Business Manager of the Hospital who was also the Dispenser and main Translator for the Hospital. A Laboratory Assistant carried out blood counts, examined the sputum and urine and looked for Malarial Parasites. The first man with a large goitre and breathing problems had walked for seven days to get to the Hospital and although she warned him he might die, and that she had never done such a difficult operation, he was still prepared to undergo it. It was a success and after three days he said he had to go home. In Britain, at that time, patients having similar surgery were kept in for 14 days.

She could turn her hand to anything that she came across and used bamboo from the forest to make splints and stretchers if she came across an injury to the limbs following trauma on her travels with jeeps to outlying clinics. Days were long and full. She got up at 5:30-6:00 am and went to bed at 10:00 pm. Visits to ill patients were followed by prayers and a daily talk with the Business Manager regarding laundry, cleaning windows, cutting grass, repairs; these duties eventually being taken over by the Business Manager. Breakfast followed and at 8:30 am she lectured to Nurses. Then at 9:30 she was operating or taking outpatients. On Saturdays she went to the main town Aizawl to do a clinic.

She returned home for the first time after nine years and was very thin. This was the first time I saw her for at that time I was a medical student in Cardiff and she gave us a talk about her life in Durtlang. My abiding impression was awe, that this young woman with fine features had been able to achieve so much in such trying conditions. When she came home next in the 1950's there was no qualified Medical staff left in the Hospital, but the following time a retired Doctor and his wife covered her work. Later, she found it easier to fly home for three month periods of leave rather than having a year away.

In 1955 on a trip to Wales she raised enough money to construct an Isolation Ward for TB patients. In 1958 due to efforts of women of the Church in Wales and Mizoram an X-ray machine was purchased and commissioned. Before this, patients had to travel 100 miles to be X-rayed. They had no blood transfusion and made solutions for intravenous use themselves. She was the only Doctor until the last four years of her time in Mizoram.

Gwyneth told me that she thought the two most important things she did there was making the Hospital part of the local Church and the training of Nurses so that the work could be carried on when she left. She succeeded in getting the Presbyterian Church in Mizoram to appoint a Hospital Board and at the opening of the X-ray Department transferred the deeds of the Hospital from the Church in Wales to the Church in Assam, so that on independence the Hospital was not foreign owned but belonged to them. She felt they knew the local conditions better than foreigners and in fact they still own it and manage it.

When she started in Durtlang, girls of 14 years old were accepted as Nurses, many of whom couldn't read or write. Gwyneth and Gwladys Evans, the Matron, started training them as part of Church work and the Hospital became a recognised training school as soon as nurse training became recognised in Assam.

Gwladys Evans had arrived in March 1936 with a great interest in public health and Gwyneth told me she was as good as a doctor and did pioneer work in the villages. She and Gwyneth had the same vision and zeal and developed a formal nursing course of four years on the pattern of the syllabus in Great Britain, and this remained the only Nursing School in Mizoram until 1981. The Assam Nursing Council devised the syllabus and examinations. The Council wrote the questions in English which she translated into Mizo – the questions were answered in Mizo which then had to be translated back to English so that they could be marked. She produced a set of

Nurses Textbooks in Mizo with the aid of the Business Manager.

She and Gwladys Evans were good teachers who taught 'first principles' training for Nurses who had to return to work in distant villages. Now there are three BSc's who do nurse training. Classes have grown from four to six nurses to 15-20 with an extension of 200 beds.

For her work in Mizoram, Gwyneth was awarded the Kaiser –I– Hind Bronze Medal. Her father had been awarded the Gold Medal for his work on behalf of the people of the plains during great floods.

Over a quarter of a century after she left, she returned having been invited back to Durtlang as a guest of honour for the opening of a new Hospital on the 12th December 1988. The dedication ceremony was combined with the Diamond Jubilee celebration of the Presbyterian Church Synod Hospital. From small beginnings in the Theological College it had grown to 200 beds, eight doctors and 70 trained nurses to serve the population of Aizawl. Miss May Bounds of Chester who followed Gwladys Evans as Matron and was there for 20 years also was a guest of honour. She and Gwladys Evans have written a book – Medical Mission to Mizoram – a story of two Nursing Sisters in a Third World Christian Hospital.

I have gone in to some detail about Gwyneth's life in India for I know that it meant a great deal to her and her work there was a great achievement. Perhaps her early years of being separated from her parents had given her independence and the will to stand on her own feet. She always made light of her academic achievements, telling me she had been lucky to have passed to become a Doctor, but she was intelligent and practical and if machinery arrived in the Hospital she would read the instructions and put it together to work. An example of this was the X-ray machine. She wasn't daunted by anything and had a commanding presence but didn't force her views and Christian beliefs on anyone.

I knew her from the time she returned to look after her parents in Prestatyn in 1962 until the end of her life in 2007. In 1994 she had travelled back to Durtlang for another celebration of the Mizoram Gospel Centenary 1894-1994 on a theme 'Gospel for All' held in an auditorium seating over 55,000 with an equal number outside, and went with some trepidation. She realised it would be tiring as well as painful to leave again such good friends she had made there. It had been a joyful time but she was very tired on her return.

It must have been very difficult for her in 1962 to come looking for work in the local hospitals when she was such an experienced Doctor in so many fields. It was a time when North Clwyd did not have a District General Hospital, but a Consultant Service was provided in 7 local Hospitals and the towns also had small Cottage Hospitals as they were called then – Community Hospitals now. Junior Medical Staff were in short supply with many coming from old commonwealth countries. To have someone like Gwyneth coming to ask for work was a tremendous help to us and she became a Clinical Assistant with sessions in Orthopaedics and Anaesthetics. She coped easily with a different way of working and getting up to date in the newer techniques of Anaesthesia. Also, she didn't mind doing night duty and being part of the emergency rota which was a big help. Her expertise and experience was eventually recognised in 1974 when she became a fulltime Medical Assistant – a specialist in Anaesthesia after a lengthy procedure through various Committees and the Welsh Office. She of course took a great interest in the surgery which was carried out and would occasionally pass comments, not always pleasing the Surgeon.

She thought the standard of asepsis was higher in India as they did not have antibiotics to treat infection so had to be very strict in maintaining sterility. She was appalled to find in one Theatre that sterilized instruments were carried through the Anaesthetic Room to get to the Theatre such was the configuration of the rooms. When she enquired why instruments were not packeted, the Sister was surprised to be told that in India this was done to protect the instruments. Eventually we had this system in Rhyl when all instruments were sterilised in a Central Sterilizing Department.

In Rhyl there was no Fly Swatter and more waste. A pack of dressings was opened and maybe only one used and then the rest thrown away. In India everything was re-sterilized. I am writing of a time almost 50 years ago – times have changed.

She continued working until 31st October 1977 then did some locum work to cover staff holidays until she was 70 years old, when she gave up clinical work. She had regularly worked in the War Memorial Hospital, HM Stanley Hospital, North Wales Hospital for Nervous Diseases and the Royal Alexandra Hospital; doing sessions elsewhere when needed as well as giving dental anaesthesia in Dentists' Surgeries.

For someone not easily frightened I remember her telling me of a scary journey following a Police Car down the middle of the old road between Abergele and Colwyn Bay to do an emergency in Colwyn Bay Hospital. With sirens loudly proclaiming their presence the Police Car set a cracking pace and she had been told to stick right behind it. When they got to the Hospital she told her passenger to get out and take the special instruments in to be sterilised whilst she sat in the car and collected her wits.

During this period of her life she had been Guardian to three children whose parents were Missionaries. On one occasion we had taken our respective children to the open-air swimming baths in Denbigh on a typical summer's day. The children had a great time and Gwyneth, not to be outdone, decided she would go in. I couldn't take my clothes off let alone get in to the water, but Gwyneth climbed to the top of the slide, held her nose and slid. She did admit afterwards that it had been very cold.

She ran a Youth Club on an estate near Penmorfa School and took some of the children for holidays. I think she enjoyed the company of children and young people. Later, when she was Chairman of Clwyd Alyn Housing Association, I went with her to one of the Hostels where she seemed quite at home talking to them.

She joined the Samaritans in Rhyl before she retired. The first meeting was convened by the Council of Churches in 1973 in Princes Street and Gwyneth became the Secretary of the Foundation Group. The Probation Officer for the area had got the Group together as there was a need and had suggested that the Council of Churches made a start. Gwyneth became the Administrator and later used her listening skills to take telephone calls. They started in the Industrial Area until they acquired an office in a Convalescent Home in Bedford Street.

Later they formed a Steering Committee. Gwyneth had definite ideas with which many did not agree. She would push these to the limit and upset people, but, she was a willing horse who would stay late if someone dropped out of the rota through illness. Gwyneth would take her knitting, a hobby she was never without, and would be happy sitting and listening to telephone calls. The day was divided into four hourly shifts and the rota included being on at night once a month and during the day once a week. At first, duty included being on duty all night, but now it has changed to two shifts a night. There could be long periods when everything was quiet and some felt the service was a waste of time. Two people did duty together and before they went off duty they would report to a Day leader by telephone who was responsible for the Centre that day. Cases of concern were reported and a return telephone call could be made to them if they wished. Some were glad of this whilst others didn't want it. Statistics were kept in a confidential manner. Gwyneth was very supportive, down to earth and had a no-nonsense attitude to the problems encountered.

Training for members was provided on a Sunday from 10:00 am to 4:00 pm when new staff were told of the calls they might encounter and this was followed by weekly evening sessions for six weeks of preparation and role play. They had social evenings and also held an Annual General Meeting, so that eventually members got to know everyone. Gwyneth was always interested and clued up and was very hurt and upset late 2001 to early 2002 as she was told she would have to retire as they couldn't get insurance for her.

She would have been prepared to carry on without their insurance but it was not to be.

She had given many talks to various community groups which afterwards would be split in two for questions with another volunteer helping her. The number of volunteers is diminishing as specialist organisations such as AA and CRUSE have taken over some of their previous calls.

They had to undertake fund raising and Gwyneth was in her element, helping with this aspect. Despite being a staunch Welsh Presbyterian she enjoyed doing pub trawls and getting money from inebriated customers near closing time. Gwyneth was solid and had humour, enjoying the company of the young with whom she had an affinity. She was indomitable and people got very fond of her once they understood her. When she was 90 they gave her a birthday party in the Centre.

She was involved in the activities of her local Church – Rehobath Presbyterian Chapel in Prestatyn – preaching, joining Women's Groups and meetings, taking Sunday School after she retired from the NHS and was Secretary of the Council of Churches in Prestatyn for fifteen years working tirelessly to bring closer liaison between the different Churches. She successfully brought together the Catholics and Pentecostals for one united service a month, a united carol service and a united Easter Service. On Maundy Thursday they have communion together and then carry a large cross up the hill behind the town where they erect it and have it flood-lit. On Easter morning they start a service around the cross at 6:30 am and by the end of the service they see the dawn breaking before going down the hill to the Church Hall to have hot cross buns. Through the Council of Churches, they staged Religious Musicals which were great fun and brought the community together.

She helped to raise interest in the Mission Field and collect money for its activities. She was one of the driving forces in getting Bishop Desmond Tutu to come to Llanelwedd for the celebration of Teulu Duw – God's Family – which was a large ecumenical gathering.

Through her work with Churches and their quest to find a role for the Churches to be involved in the local community she helped to set up a Citizen's Advice Bureau in Prestatyn and was the first Chairman.

She became concerned about the plight of the homeless and those who were sleeping rough and through the Samaritans she was asked to attend a meeting in the Westminster Hotel, Rhyl to discuss the possibility in conjunction with the Housing Corporation of setting up a Housing Association in North Wales. This was in the Autumn of 1978 and she remembered having tea with cucumber sandwiches with six others who met a representative from the Welsh Office. Gwyneth and Eurwen Edwards were two of the seven who attended and who became Founder Members of Clwyd Alyn Housing Association. Garden City Estate in Queensferry was handed over to them in 1979 by Collingwood Housing Association in England. They appointed an Executive Officer and started developing social housing. A Management Board was formed and she became involved in all aspects of the work becoming in 1993 the Chairman and on her retirement, President.

She was honoured with an MBE in the Birthday Honours of 1996 for her services to the community, and so had been recognised by both countries in which she had left her mark. Although I knew her well I had never asked her the questions I have asked the other women Doctors who are still alive.

I doubt that she had any regrets as she had been an achiever in so many ways. She was a negotiator and peace maker, thinking war was wrong and consensus should be reached to avoid it. Although she told me that she had not had a religious experience, she was in every way a Christian. In many ways a visionary – she could see what needed doing and got on with it. She liked children and had the experience of being a Foster Parent. She would I feel have liked children of her own and regarded the Chief Executive of Clwyd Alyn very much as a son. She had humour, made pithy comments, had an infectious laugh and was great fun enjoying the company of men especially those who weren't frightened of her and would tease her. We always spoke Welsh together.

She had cared for her parents at home, her father dying in his 90's and her mother a centenarian. Her last years were trying as she eventually had to go into a Nursing Home, where her eagle eye spotted everything and she wasn't prepared to put up with shoddy standards. She never complained and was grateful to her legion of friends who called regularly to see her.

A pillar of society, Carer, Doctor, Missionary, firm Chairman of wise counsel, she used all the talents which she'd been given to help others. Looking back on her life she was proud of her achievements in Mizoram and also what she had been able to do in a voluntary capacity when she came home to Wales, including ecumenism.

I think life taught her not to be afraid to tackle what others may think are insurmountable. She thought that perseverance and determination will help you find ways to tackle problems. Her philosophy was to find a way to keep peace not war.

Chapter Twelve

Dr Aileen Mary Hampton MBBS, MRCS LRCP
[3 May 1925 – 12 July 2010]
First Cytologist
Associate Specialist

Aileen found a niche for herself in North Clwyd by setting up the Cytology service for the district. She had met Edward Parry-Jones who became her husband when they were both working in the Liverpool Maternity Hospital. He was appointed Consultant Obstetrician and Gynaecologist in 1952 and had his unit in St Asaph General Hospital, later to be renamed HM Stanley Hospital in 1959. Aileen was pregnant with their first child when they arrived and they lived first in rooms in the Nurses' home at the hospital and moved later to Plas yn Roe Cottage on the Glascoed Road until they moved into their home, 'Trefelwy', Mount Road, St Asaph in 1954. This was a large family home with outbuildings and a large garden where Aileen could enjoy creating a beautiful garden and Edward enjoy renovating old cars.

Aileen was born in the Isle of Man, one of two daughters of a

Medical Practitioner, Percy William Hampton [1876-1967] and his wife, Margaret Ann ("Daisy"). She was educated at the Buchan School, Castletown and then proceeded to the Royal Free Hospital where her friends from that time were Phyllis George, the first woman to be Vice-President of the Royal College of Surgeons and Wendy Clarke who became a Consultant Anaesthetist. Aileen qualified with Honours and was awarded a mark of distinction in Applied Pharmacology and Therapeutics. Her sister, Geraldine, also became a Medical Practitioner.

Her father was a Consultant Surgeon in Douglas. He graduated MBChB in 1899 from Edinburgh University having won the Bronze Medal for Anatomy and became a Demonstrator in Anatomy, his favourite subject. He was a House Surgeon at the Devonshire Hospital, Buxton for two years before going to South Africa as a Civil Surgeon in the South African Field Force 1901-02. He gained an MD in 1905 on Osteoarthritis. He became Assistant Surgeon at Noble's Isle of Man Hospital whilst at the same time being a General Practitioner as was common at the time. To recuperate following surgery in 1912/13 he did a trip as Ship's Surgeon to the Far East and West Coast of North America. He joined the RAMC 1917/18 becoming a Major and was a Specialist Surgeon at the Military Hospital, Ripon Reserve Centre. Aileen probably got her interest in Medicine from him. Strangely, she didn't like patients which must have influenced her in her eventual speciality. This is reflected in her job at Liverpool where she carried out post-mortems. She qualified in 1948 and on 1st July she was appointed a House Surgeon in Pathology at Lawn Road Annex to the Royal Free Hospital for a year. She was considered for the Helen Prideaux Scholarship in 1949 and in January 1950 she became a Registrar Pathologist at the United Liverpool Hospitals based at Liverpool Maternity Hospital, with occasional duties in the Women and Children's Hospitals. It was here that she carried out post-mortems including babies. Within six months she was engaged and by September 1950 married to Edward. They had three children; 2 boys and a girl – Cennydd in 1952, Michael in 1954 and Carolyn in 1955.

After they moved to Trefelwy she would help Edward with his private practice being a chaperone, nurse and technician. In 1959 she started attending the Dermatology Department as a Clinical Assistant in Rhyl, but on Dr Emslie's appointment in 1962 she relinquished this. It was in the early 1960's that Aileen started working in the Pathology Laboratory in HM Stanley Hospital reporting on Cervical Smears. In 1966 she trained in Cervical Cytology in the Gynaecology/Pathology Department of Liverpool University and was then appointed on 15th June 1966 for 12 hours per week, graded as Basic Grade – Biochemist, until April 1974 when she became a Clinical Assistant for 10½ hours per week in the Pathology Department at the Royal Alexandra Hospital, Rhyl. Eventually in 1975 she was appointed an Associate Specialist running the Cytology Service for North Clwyd. She had started her early interest in Cytology under the guidance of Dr Tim Alban-Lloyd and had developed her skills with meticulous attention to detail. She attended meetings of the Association of Cytologists of Great Britain and also hosted a national meeting of the Association in Glan Clwyd Hospital a year before she retired.

Aileen attended an advanced course in Cytology in Manchester in 1973 and in that year became a Family Planning Medical Officer, carrying out clinics as far away as Bangor and she had started lectures for Family Planning Courses in Liverpool to doctors and nurses.

She attended meetings of the Medical Women's Federation and in November 1973, when Catrin Williams was President, she was on the organising committee when the Council visited Prestatyn.

She was bright, intelligent, pretty, with dark curly hair, fine features, small boned, height 5 foot – always wore very high heels and was addicted to wearing scarves, rarely appearing without one.

They had help in the house and she was a very gracious hostess when they entertained their friends, with Edward enjoying parties. She enjoyed gardening and was also an accomplished pianist.

However, she was a very reticent person and not at all comfortable being the focus of attention. She hated having her photo taken, but liked photography. She would only really play the piano for herself and rarely for anyone else. She enjoyed gardening, but often this appeared to be a form of academic interest rather than the aim to create a beautiful garden. In other words, there was more for her in the growing of a particular plant rather than the outcome of its aesthetic appeal in the garden position.

She published an article "Growing up with Gardens" for the North Wales Gardener – Volume 24 which is the Journal of the North Wales Horticultural Society about her passion for gardens and gardening and her great good fortune to be associated with enthusiastic gardeners and a wide variety of gardens throughout her life. In this she pays tribute to her parents for teaching her about the countryside, plants and trees. She writes well and know-ledgably about gardens in the Isle of Man where she grew up, Exeter where she found herself for a year as a 17 year old student, London, Stowe and Amersham.

After she retired in 1990 she attended local history study groups and also studied spiders scientifically, reading a considerable amount about them as there were plenty to study in Trefelwy. She enjoyed history, was a Welcomer with Edward in St Asaph Cathedral, and was interested in the History of Medicine.

Although her nature was reticent, private and shy she had a tremendous belief in her role as a supporter for Edward and put her own career second to this task. You could perhaps say this was from a huge sense of duty and from this stemmed a huge admiration of the Queen. If she had not married Edward, and if she had followed her own career, then she would have been academically brilliant, but whether she would have had the "political elbows" to get to the top in what was a very male dominated profession in the 1950's/60's her son was unable to say.

She had a bad car crash in the late 1950's early 1960's caused by black ice near Brookes' field between Rhyl and Rhuddlan in her black Morris 8 and she suffered from Migraines. She later had a hip replacement and entered a Nursing Home in St Asaph.

She supported her husband to the end and some days before Edward's sudden death, she hosted a Sunday lunch party, to which we were invited and where he had a "funny turn" and the ambulance service attended. However, after he recovered he carried on being his jovial self and she produced delicious desserts. The "show" went on.

Chapter Thirteen

June Lilian Churchman OBE, DL, BSc, DipEd
[1927-2009]

An incident which had the greatest effect on June, when she was six years old, occurred when she was listening to a radio programme of a Christmas Appeal for children. She had been nurtured in a happy secure home in Birmingham, the middle child in a widely spaced family of three children who were all well fed and well cared for. The programme was an appeal to help poor unhappy children and described an alien world to hers, which she found difficult to comprehend. Theirs was not a family to display their emotions, but she was so shaken by what she heard that she left the room to go to her bedroom as she was so upset. Her mother followed her and June asked her if it was true that there were poor unhappy children in the world as the thought had never occurred to her. It was an eye-opener into the world of the needy.

Her mother was generous with time for charitable works and would visit young women in Birmingham who were poor. June would accompany her with gifts of household helpful items such as soap. This instilled in her the urge to be helpful and in the years which followed she looked after her family through illness and infirmity.

They did not have household help when she was a child and she was expected to help her mother, to be orderly and tidy and keep things in their place. She was brought up with a work ethic, not to strive for honours or gains but rather to have humility. This resulted in later life in surprise when she was asked to undertake tasks and when she gained honours. She enjoyed meeting people and was always looking for ways and opportunities to be helpful and improve.

She was born on 23rd June 1927 to George and Lilian Ball in Birmingham. Her brother, Dennis, was eight years older and now lives in Minorca. Her sister, Patricia, was eight years younger and although they did not meet often, her death in 2007 was a shock for June. Her father was a Patton Maker for the big cars manufactured in Birmingham and he and his wife were great dancers and brought the Tango to Blackpool. He retired when he was 47 years old because of ill-health and consequently had to sell their home to get an income from the proceeds. He was fortunate to get paid work as a Parish Clerk which had a large tied house; which at one time had been a Headmasters House; into which they moved as a family. During this time he ran dancing classes for charity which were popular and gave him an added interest. Her mother did not have to gain employment.

After primary school June was educated at George Dixon's Grammar School where she became Head Girl in 1946 and captained the tennis and netball teams, showing early leadership qualities. She was offered a place at the Royal Holloway College in London to read Mathematics and Biology but family circumstances changed and consequently she remained at home to help her mother and gained a Teachers Scholarship to read Mathematics at Birmingham University under Professor Watson. This was in the form of a grant to help her upkeep on the understanding that when she got her degree she would continue her education to attain the Diploma in Education. She did not regret her change of course or early hopes of studying medicine, but went on to gain a Degree in Mathematics and also a Postgraduate Diploma in Psychology and Education in Professor Schonel's Department.

She met Trevor at University, where he was a Research Fellow in the Metallurgy Department. This was the start of a great partnership and he has always been a tower of strength for her, especially when later she gradually became immobile and was unable to drive or walk far.

At University she was elected to the Guild of Undergraduates Council. During one rag week she appeared twice nightly at the Aston Hippodrome in a sketch "Over The Garden Wall". Her acting talents were also used when she was teaching – as a member of staff performing in "1066 And All That". She was elected the first woman Chairman of Carnival Rag Week and gave Trevor the task of organising the procession. She raised the record sum for the time of £10,000.

On leaving University she taught first at Stourbridge High School for Girls, and then at Kendrick School in Reading after she and Trevor were married and they had bought their first house there in 1950. She gave up teaching full time when Hugh was born in 1956. Helena was born in 1959 and two months later they moved as a family to Uley, Gloucestershire when Trevor was appointed Head of the Materials Division and the Deputy Director of Berkeley Nuclear Laboratories.

June became a Supply Teacher at Catherine Lady Berkeley School at Wootten-under-Edge and also joined the Inner Wheel Club at Dursley – this being the charitable organisation for wives of Rotarians. It was made possible for her to do this as her parents came to live with them when Lilian Ball became ill. June also joined the Girl Guide Association as an adult at this time, becoming District Commissioner for Dursley, Gloucestershire. She joined the Guiding Movement when she was at School in Birmingham due to encouragement from a junior Mathematics Teacher, but it was war time and they didn't do much in this after-school activity. In 1965 Trevor was appointed the Founder Director of the Electricity Council Research Centre at Capenhurst, and they moved to live in Pantasaph, near Holywell. June transferred her Inner Wheel (IW) membership to Chester, becoming President of the Chester Club and also Chairman of IW District 18, which covered North Wales, the Wirral, Chester, Cheshire and Lancashire.

She became County Commissioner (Girl Guiding) for the original historic county of Flintshire and with the local Government re-organisation of the early 1970's, united Flintshire and Denbighshire Guide Counties into the Guide County of Clwyd with Lady Margaret Middleton as President, a role June took over some years later.

In 1975 she was an observer with the UK delegation to the World Conference of Girl Guides and Girl Scouts in England. She was appointed Deputy Chief Commissioner for Wales and in 1981 she was a member of the UK delegation to the World Conference of Girl Guides and Girl Scouts in Orleans, France. In 1985 she was appointed OBE for her services to guiding and the young people of Wales. She had always been interested in the young and had been Vice-President of CWVYS (The Council for Wales Voluntary Youth Service), a pre-Wales Assembly organisation. She was appointed Vice-President of Girl Guides Cymru and Girl Guiding UK – an honour she held until her death. She was also appointed Vice-President of Clwyd Scouts. At the beginning she did a lot with them, but not latterly. She felt that it is important to have close co-operation between the Scouts and Guides. In 1985 she was appointed Deputy Lieutenant (DL) of Clwyd, one of the first Lady Deputy Lieutenants. In an emergency she acted as a Supply Teacher in Holywell High School for a short period.

Her teaching role had been important to her throughout her life and when she was teaching full time, she felt that school could take over her life completely. She enjoyed helping children and adults to develop and get the best out of themselves and encouraged them to do this. All the organisations she has been involved with have also helped her to develop. She always tried to devise new methods of doing things to stop her audience and herself from getting bored. A different approach was challenging and stimulating to keep the subject fresh and she had three or four methods she played with in order to promote discussion and draw out relevant points. She thought that Helena, her daughter, has the same approach and is also an excellent teacher. She also found satisfaction in the charitable social side of her life; of being involved with people to raise money for charitable causes.

In 1994/5 she was asked to chair the Appeal Committee to raise money to restore the organ in the Cathedral Church of St Asaph. This was an exhausting task but one where her networking and organisational flair came to the fore, so that she had the satisfaction of seeing an organ valued at £1.7 million at its final restoration.

Her final, and surprising to her, appointment was as one of the Welsh Representatives on the newly formed National Lotteries Charity Board, chaired by Sir David Sieff. In 1994 she met a number of very influential people and I remember her telling me that she liked strong men and that it was a very good Board at the beginning. She enjoyed the discussions and reading the supporting comments to the applications for grants. Many on the Board "couldn't see the wood for the trees" and occasionally she helped with training. In those five challenging years she was "one of the few on the Board with real experience of squeezing blood out of a stone". Although she had always striven to improve the life of women she hadn't experienced any glass ceiling to break through and couldn't see any barrier to women achieving that she would like to see removed.

I had met June through the Wales Assembly of Women (WAW) which was good when it was initially set up but it petered out and became far too "southern orientated". The North-South divide certainly took its toll and the northern voice sidelined. June became

Vice-Chairman and the organisation would have been quite different if she had become Chairman. Interestingly, June did not mention WAW until I questioned her about it. Neither did she mention her Church activities or beliefs. She helped St Asaph Cathedral as I have mentioned, and when she and Trevor moved to Dodleston in 2001 because of her declining health and mobility, she again became involved with others in raising money to restore the Church Tower. Also, she took part in intercessions during services once a month for 2-3 years, and was a member of the Parish Church Council.

June had always been family orientated. When her mother became ill with cancer shortly after Trevor and June had moved to Gloucestershire, her parents came to live with them as her father also had a chronic illness. After her mother's death aged 73 years, her father continued to live in the flat attached to their home, dying at the age of 88 years. Her mother's sister also lived with them and she died aged 95 years, although for the last 3 years she had lived in a Nursing Home.

As well as her children, Hugh and Helena, she has four grandchildren – Christina, Nikola, Alexandra and Christian, all of whom were baptised in St Asaph Cathedral. Her grandchildren are not academic but she got on well with them all.

June has had a very full and interesting life and has happy memories. One especially lovely experience was being invited to a Reception on the Royal Yacht which was berthed in Liverpool in 1977.

Her life is even more remarkable in the way she has coped with illness as well, over the last 30 years or so. She has an air of stoical quiet acceptance and has never questioned "why me"? Rather she has gone on to cope with it, coming to terms with it; "there is no point in grumbling all the time". She was diagnosed with Multiple Sclerosis (MS) in 1980, which was Type 3 – meaning that it would be a slow and manageable decline. In Pantasaph they had a large family home and garden which she loved and was happy being outside working in it. When everything became too much to do, they moved to Dodleston to a bungalow. After a life of service to others she became the recipient of little things others did for her such as cutting of toe nails, sewing etc.

Multiple Myeloma, a cancer of the bones, was diagnosed in 2006 and her doctors gave up predicting when she might die. She was advised not to have surgery because of cardiac conduction problems, resulting in an irregular heart beat and attempted chemotherapy reactivated her MS. However, treatment with a massive blood transfusion and other therapy brought the Multiple Myeloma under control, but at a cost.

She had two nasty falls which had shaken her and a third fall resulted in a fracture of the femur. This necessitated a general anaesthetic which she survived, and the wound healed without infection. She returned home to Trevor who did the cooking and shopping. They had help on some days and although she slept a lot as a result of medication, she was able to get out of bed for part of each day.

When I asked June what life had taught her she told me "not to expect too much and not to make instant judgements". It was important to listen, to question, to weigh things up before making decisions, but if she felt strongly about something, it was important to have a strong voice. "Say as little as you need until everyone has had their say and then discuss". "Don't expect the impossible, be patient and never give in".

June died in the Hospice of the Good Shepherd Backford at 2:30 am on Monday, 22nd June 2009, the day before her 82nd birthday, and her funeral service was held in St Mary's Church, Dodleston the following Friday, the 26th. The church was full and the flower arrangements perfect in various shades of pink, with a single wreath of pink flowers on the coffin. The Reverend Jackie Kendal took the service, having been given permission to do so by the incumbent as she had promised June two years previously that she would officiate. She spoke of June's love of life, love of the church and love of God, and gave a memorable reading of the words we know so well from 1. Corinthians, Chapter 13 – "faith, hope and love and the greatest of these is love". Helena had given an eulogy of her mother's life which June had written. Her granddaughter and Marion read a poem and the Reverend Jackie brought out June's astuteness, wisdom, her love of owls, her quiet determination, her banter with Trevor and her care and compassion for her fellow man and woman. Huw and Helena with their spouses Marion and Simon carried her coffin, shoulder high, out to the churchyard where she was buried with only her immediate family present. A remarkable woman having a fitting service at the end in a village church.

A service of thanksgiving for her life organised by the Girl Guides was held in November in St Asaph Cathedral.

Eurwen Holland Edwards OBE, BEM
[21st February 1920 -   ]

Eurwen has a great love of life which she maintains keeps her going in this her 91st year. "I'm alive – it's lovely" has been her lifelong philosophy, and she has been lucky to have had a strong constitution which has enabled her to continue serving others. She likes having her say, doesn't want anything to go on without knowing about it, loves interfering and has an inbred need to help. She wishes she had met Mother Teresa and would have liked to have gone to India to see how she had coped.

She has no regrets about marrying young or not moving away

from Rhyl and is still contributing to her community and to Wales. For her great contribution as a Volunteer and services to the community she was honoured with an OBE in 2009.

Her father was the greatest influence on her life and had been a very good man. He taught her to treat everyone with respect and to be polite. She would follow him everywhere and in St Asaph Parish Church when he read the lesson, she would sit on the Vicar's knee. People would come to him for advice and he was regarded as the poor man's lawyer. After his death in 1931 when she was 11 years old her mother paid to have improved lighting installed above the lectern, to assist the readers. She had perfect Welsh when her father was alive but afterwards lost it, although now it is returning.

John Williams Wynne, her father [1878-1931] was said to be illegitimate. He understood that his father had been a Sea Captain who was married to a Lady and that on his birth his mother had given him to a gardener's wife to be wet nursed and subsequently he had been fostered by them. The gardener was a Wynne and the child brought up as John Wynne. However, despite her father having gone to Somerset House he was unable to find out a connection with the Williams Wynne family who were gentry and landowners in North Wales. The Archbishop of Wales would meet her from School and told her that one day he would tell her what the connection was, but didn't do so. His obituary, in the Rhyl Journal, indicates he was the son of John Elidan Wynne and born in Ellesmere, Shropshire.

John Wynne had attended St Asaph Boys Grammar School and left aged fourteen years to become a postman in St Asaph. He also became a scribe for the First Archbishop of Wales, who led the Church to independence – Alfred George Edwards [1848-1937], so obviously had demonstrated good writing skills. When he was a boy he was a member of the St Asaph Cathedral Choir at the same time as the boy who later wrote the well known World War I song – "Pack Up Your Troubles In Your Old Kit Bag!".

In 1914 he was called up, joining the Army in Earl Haig's

Expeditionary Force and being deployed in administrative duties involving his calligraphy.

John Wynne married Myfanwy Thomas of St Asaph. Eurwen's maternal grandmother, Mary Thomas, came from Denbigh and her grandfather, Henry Thomas, from Cefnmeiriadog where he was a country postman. They had three sons and four daughters After their marriage John and Myfanwy lived in Tegfan in Mount Road, St Asaph and after John Wynne died they moved in with her grandmother, Mary Thomas, in Bronwylfa Square, where Mary was a national telephonist, her home being the Telephone Exchange.

John and Myfanwy had two daughters, their younger daughter Mary Eilidian being four years younger than Eurwen and they had a happy, secure childhood. Eurwen had been christened with water from the river Jordan. She remembers salmon boxes in the river Elwy being blown up by poachers and also she remembers skating on the frozen river Clwyd in winter below Bronwylfa, a big house on the outskirts of St Asaph.

When Eurwen was nine years old she was given a birthday treat by an uncle of an aeroplane flight around Rhyl from Dyserth Road, telling me there had been no time to feel ill. Her mother's sister, Gwladys, married the first man from Rhyl to be honoured with the Military Medal. He was Edward Ellis, known as Ted. Two of her relatives were admitted to Penyffordd, Meadowslea Hospital for Tuberculosis and she remembers the wide open windows there which formed part of the treatment – giving clean fresh air. Another uncle ran away with a patient and was not allowed to return to the hospital, a typical response following a misdemeanour in a TB Hospital at that time. This uncle trained a dog to get on the bus at the bottom of St Asaph High Street hill and get off at the top.

When she was a child her father took her with him when he visited St Asaph Workhouse and taught her "no-one is better than me, and I am no better than them". There was a chalk circle with a dot in the middle of the path outside their home which informed tramps that cups of tea were available there. Her father had been given a book called "Memories about Churches" and signed Gerald Cambrensis – To John Wynne.

Eurwen attended the National School and after passing the scholarship examination, moved to St Asaph Grammar School where she was allowed free books to study. She enjoyed sport and played hockey for the school, but following a knock on her kidney she had surgery in Denbigh Infirmary and although she didn't lose her kidney, she was off school for a year and then became a telephonist. She regarded this lost year as the biggest trauma of her life at the time when it should have been one of the best years. She lost friends and her first boyfriend who did not return from fighting in World War II who were irreplaceable, but her philosophy has been to remember the good times not dwell on the bad.

During World War II her mother was War Occupation Sister with the VAD at Kinmel Camp and would invite young men back to the house for tea and Sunday meals. When Eurwen got married they all walked from the Camp to St Asaph to stand outside the Parish Church to see her.

Eurwen met her husband, Gwilym, through his brother Edwyn who was a telephonist and who invited her to meet them in 1939. Gwilym was in the Home Guard in 1940 and they married in 1941. He was No. 2 in the LDF – Local Defence Force – which then became the Home Guard. Gwilym's father was an Estate Agent and Valuer in Rhyl and became unwell during the war, whereupon Eurwen helped him to run the business until Gwilym came out of the Army and took it on. She told me that the business taught her to be diplomatic and to see the other person's point of view, and she looked back on it as a very happy time. During the war years, she was also involved in the placement of evacuees in homes.

Gwilym's father was a great Labour man whilst hers was Conservative, and through this connection she met many eminent men of their day – Shinwell, Morrison who stayed with them; Royston Griffiths and Attlee. Her father-in-law met Churchill in London and heard him speak, telling her it was the best speech he had ever heard. They met Attlee in Nefyn and she told him to tell her father to hurry up as she was fed up with waiting. David, her son, met them all.

David was born in 1943 in St Asaph. He attended Fairhome School then, when the family moved to Rhyl, he went to Rhyl Grammar School. Afterwards he joined the Friends Provident Insurance, which was Quaker based, and had very good training with them before moving to the Midland Bank which became the HSBC gaining the position of Head of Sales Training and remaining there until he retired; afterwards doing consultancy work. Pauline, his wife, works for the Friends Provident in Manchester. Eurwen has a high regard for her as a considerate daughter-in-law and marvellous wife. David and Pauline had twins – a girl Sian and boy Matthew. Sian trained as a Teacher in Bangor and Matthew became a Nuclear Physicist in Manchester University.

Eurwen did voluntary duty at the Nuffield Centre in Kinmel Park Camp during World War II, where National Service Training was carried out. Matthew Jones, Headmaster of Rhyl Grammar School looked after the boys and she looked after the girls. If their relatives came to Rhyl, she would help them find accommodation.

She joined the WRVS in 1961 because she had helped with billeting during the war. She started with the meals on wheels service. She was fond of people and started the club for the elderly for the WRVS in Rhyl. Then, again for the WRVS, she became Emergency Services Officer for Flintshire. There they carried out exercises in an underground station in Mold.

In 1974 she became Clwyd County Organiser which included Colwyn, Wrexham, Conwy, Rhos-on-Sea, Flintshire and Denbighshire, and carried this out until 1985.

She opened 74 WRVS Clubs in her day, with most having become self-supporting. She was honoured with the British Empire Medal for this work. Old people would pass on their skills to the young, eg crochet and tatting. She became Chair of Clwyd Voluntary Services Council in 1970 and regarded this as a big family, knew everyone and the needs of the elderly and disabled. When Clwyd was divided it meant vying for everything and she hopes with re-organisation it will go back to one area. Eurwen served on the Clwyd Family Practitioner Committee (FPC) remaining from the start until re-organisation, becoming Vice-Chairman, and was Chair of the Medical Service Committee for 4 years.

She is Chair of Age Concern for North Wales Central and is a Trustee for the Rhyl Coast Credit Union. She was asked to go to the inaugural meeting of Clwyd Alyn Housing Association in October 1978 because of her link with the voluntary services and also her concern for housing for the elderly for 30 years. Charles Hogg was on the first Committee with Dr Gwyneth Roberts, Dr Janet Williams from Colwyn Bay, Mr Kitto a Councillor and Reverend Trevor Davies in the Chair. Ron Dixon joined later and became Chair.

She has given continuous, unstinting service to Clwyd Alyn Housing Association, Tŷ Glas Housing Society and the Pennaf Housing Group since 1978, and in recognition of all her devotion and support she has been President of the Group since 2007. For her outstanding community work, over the last 50 years, she was presented with a unique special tribute at a prestigious Care Forum Wales Award Ceremony in Cardiff for her significant and lasting contribution to the Voluntary Sector in Wales in 2007. The presentation was made by the Welsh Assembly Deputy Minister for Health and Social Services, Gwenda Thomas.

She is Vice-President of Denbighshire Voluntary Services and has seen big changes in the last 45 years, with fewer volunteers to help with Saturday morning activities as more women are now working. People are too busy to listen and pick on the bad things instead of publicising the good things of the young. "The more you do the younger you feel" and "help someone as you walk along" are part of her philosophy. She feels she has "lived in the best times"

She worked well with Vera Russell Hughes of the Red Cross, wife of a General Practitioner in Rhyl, to bring their joint service to the community. They also attended big training exercises outside

Wrexham in Nesscliffe and learnt a lot from them. She and her team from WRVS cleaned a reception area in Towyn Camp in the late 1970's for the reception of black mothers and babies escaping Idi Amin's tyranny in Africa. The mothers handed the babies through the train windows in Towyn to the waiting WRVS helpers and they then had the task of finding and reuniting them. They had cleaned the camp before their arrival scouring toilets with brillo pads. She learnt a lot on feeding and clothing in this very big camp. The children were only allowed to bring one toy.

She feels more can be done to help vulnerable people for the first six weeks on their return home from hospital. The Red Cross organise a team of volunteers to telephone or visit them. This is a new service which should be promoted and extended from a new centre with a team who can carry out domestic duties and shop as well as chat. She has been Chair of the Health Alliance.

She formed and was the Conductor of a choir of 150/200 elderly people who visited Homes to sing old songs, which proved to be very popular. She organised keep fit classes in the club for the elderly at the Old People's Centre in Vale Road, where lunch was provided every day and provided the base for the meals on wheels service.

The Club for the Elderly in Vale Road, Rhyl put on a "This is your Life" show with Mr Silvey who had worked as a Cabin Boy during the War. Tapes of this were made and are kept in Rhyl Library as well as a Ration Book with lovely writing in it by Mr Silvey. There are also tapes of the choir singing at different events and pantomimes. Anne Zieglar and Webster Booth sang for them in the Wrexham Club.

She enjoyed organising pantomimes in Rhyl in the Club, which were hilarious affairs and recalls in one a bucket of water was aimed at her from the stage which missed her had drenched the Mayor.

When Glan Clwyd Hospital opened she started the Reception services with WRVS, also the Hospital Trolley Service; later starting a similar service at the new Maelor Hospital in Wrexham. When the

War Memorial Hospital in Rhyl closed, she started the Reception Service at the Royal Alexandra Hospital.

Working in the Nuffield Centre in Kinmel Park brought the problems of the young to her attention. She has always been interested in football, supporting Manchester United, Liverpool and Wales, and this she found helped her to talk to them.

Through her attachment to Clwyd Alyn and WCVA, she was aware of the problems of insolvency. Mr Haydn Rees – Chief Executive of Clwyd C.C. and Dr John Chapman influenced and helped her a great deal. She had her office in Llwyn Egrin Hall and would meet Mr Rees there.

She has not allowed disappointments to rule her life, but is concerned that youngsters and the elderly are often not able to achieve. She is not lonely, has had good health and takes ill health as it comes. She has not allowed her husband's illness to stand in her way and has learnt not to argue but to get out of the way for a short time to allow arguments to pass. Further deterioration in Gwilym's health has resulted in his admission to a Home.

She feels it is not a good thing to move from friends or family at retirement, or after loss of a partner. It is not good to live with family, but to retain independence – especially after losing a partner. "Stay where you are for a short time after a bereavement, don't run away, keep your independence and afterwards take a break".

When I asked her how she would improve the life of women, she said she wished society would find a way to help mothers stay at home if that was their wish, instead of going out to work, although she was glad that there was equal pay for women now. In her day, mother stayed at home to look after the family and was there to listen and talk to the children when they returned from school. People now have no time to stop and think and the young need a mentor. The Vicar's wife in the past was a pivotal link in the community but she now also has a job. Flexitime has been useful to mothers with children but she feels more could be done to induce them to stay at home.

Pat Francis JP, BSc [5th February 1927 – 24th December 2008]
Wife of a Dentist, Community Worker, Chairman of Welsh Ladies Golf Union

I met Ben and Pat Francis in 1955. Ben had a Dental Practice in Abergele and became a Clinical Assistant in the Maxillo-Facial Department at St Asaph General Hospital, working closely with Gordon Hardman – Consultant Surgeon. Ben was extremely dextrous in the use of his hands with the fine work and use of equipment and splints needed in the correction of severe facial injuries which were treated at St Asaph. In those early days I

anaesthetised these patients and got to know Ben and through him met his wife, Pat. Abergele was a very sociable place and I was invited to parties in their home where Ben would play the piano and Pat was an interesting conversationalist and welcoming hostess.

We maintained our friendship over the years, although we didn't meet regularly. As I was leaving Pat's room in St Kentigern's Hospice on 10th November 2008, Remembrance Sunday, she said "one may not see old friends as often as one would like, but the affection always remains". I replied "happy memories". True words and a bond. We had discussed family and the diverse lives of our children and grandchildren, the horrors of war and unbearable pathos of services of Remembrance, and as I got up I told her "you have a good memory Pat, can I write the story of your life". She readily agreed. She was concerned about the future and where she should go. I said "I'll be back soon with my notebook".

Unfortunately, by the time of my next visit it was obviously too late to impose this on her. I was unable to attend her funeral, but her family have given me a copy of the eulogy of her life they had written and I interviewed Julia, her daughter, when I learnt much about her that I didn't know.

Pat was born on 5th February 1927 to Charles Adolph and Nina Cunningham. Her father was born into a big family in the Isle of Man. During a Scarlet Fever epidemic many died including his sister. He ran away to join the Navy during World War I and was injured in Mesopotamia. When he married Nina and they had children he became a house husband looking after the family whilst his wife went out to work. Pat was their youngest child and had three older brothers. John, the eldest was nine years older, Alan, seven years older had a heart condition and was a blue baby, and Ronnie was four years older. Pat was very close to her father and loved to listen to his tales of the foreign countries he had visited. Her mother became a Nurse in Wrightington Hospital, near Wigan. When the bombing of Liverpool occurred in WWII she would try and persuade her husband and the two younger sons to move to Wigan where it was thought to be safer. Pat has written graphically of her early life as follows:

> When I was seven we moved to a house in Seaforth later to be known as Crosby – to No 68 Rawson Road, Hanover House. It was a large double-fronted house with three stories and cellars. At first we only had part of it, sharing with several other people. We had most of the two upper floors, but in one room on the first floor was a man, magical to us as children because he was an "Inventor" – particularly treasured because he had designed something for Cadbury's Chocolate ... and was a regular recipient of parcels of chocolates. Sadly, his wife suffered from what was called "Sugar Diabetes" and, to my knowledge, they had no children – so we benefited. With the selfishness of children, I only remember the chocolates, not his name (it was Lynch [October 2008]).

My eldest brother John was nine years older than I, exactly so because we shared the same birthday, 5th February. I thought him very beautiful and he was a soloist (until his voice broke) in the choir of St John's Church, Waterloo. Alan, the middle boy, was seven years older and was the main focus of attention in our family because of his major heart problems. He had been a "blue baby" and developed a vastly enlarged heart with a pigeon chest to compensate for its deficiencies. His fingers were severely clubbed. In cold weather they and his lips and cheeks would be almost black. He had short sight and I remember that he couldn't dress until he put on his glasses in the mornings. He was a clever boy, excelling in examinations but must have missed so much regular schooling because of the seemingly endless bouts of pneumonia every winter, but my mother somehow always pulled him back to life.

Ronnie, my immediate senior, was fair-haired and blue-eyed – he was the one who used to lie in wait for me on the stairs to wallop me with a cushion. It must have been galling for him to have had a sister after four years of being the baby. Still, we were good friends. I believe that my mother miscarried another child between Ronnie and me. He was a boy and she would have named him George after her father, George Adam Cunningham.

My life was filled, happily with school, Sunday School, Church – listening to my father's stories of his life in the Regular Army in India before the First World War – not so much contact with my mother then because she was our bread-winner. My father had been wounded in Mesopotamia – I suppose it would have been in about 1916. He was in the "Kings Regiment", sent there from India. He had a large shrapnel wound in his shin which broke down frequently. I believe he had Osteomyelitis - pieces of bone were always coming away, but he resisted any suggestion of amputation.

He also suffered from recurrent bouts of Malaria. So many men suffered wretched health after the First World War, particularly those who had been gassed. It was hard for the healthy to find work – virtually impossible for those with any flaw. My mother was a skilled cook and worked for several families – the one I remember best, lived in a beautiful house – "The White House" near Ira Blundell on the Southport Road. It was surrounded by large gardens and woods and mother went every day there by bus. She was known as the ladies "Companion". In holiday time I would accompany her and found it all enthralling. I don't suppose that the money could have been very much, but somehow we managed. My father, too, was a skilful cook having spent part of his Army life as Cooks Assistant to the Officers' Mess. I'm sure that we were very poor but we had good style and great imaginative stimulation from them both. My mother had trained as an Artist in the Liverpool School of Art and we had several still life paintings of hers on our walls. There were also some beautiful water colours by Richard Wilson – lovely gold mounts and frames. I wish I had them now. She used to tell me that her mother had been painted by Holman Hunt when some of the pre-Raphaelites spent some time in mid-Wales. My father was a beaver for education – he haunted our library, coming home with armfuls of books – all our meal-times were enriched with "spelling bees", general knowledge, history and debate.

So the years passed frugally but contentedly – I passed the "Scholarship" when I was 10 and also won a scholarship to the Merchant Taylors Girls School in Waterloo – but was asked to stand back for another year because I was too young. I'm glad I didn't go there because I later found that "Scholarship Girls" wore a slightly different uniform and were clearly separated from the others who paid fees! I entered Waterloo Park Secondary School for Girls in September 1937, but had to stay in the first form for two years because of my age. I don't remember feeling any resentment about this. I enjoyed being at school, particularly the Sciences, Geography, English and Art. We must have lived about two miles or more from the school and I used to walk or go on my bike. The only Teachers I really remember were Miss Hegarty – Geography and Miss Spence – English, whom I admired immensely. Strangely enough, when I was first a student at Rankin Hall in 1945 she was the Tutor in my house. In fact we shared a bathroom.

When the war began I was first entering the Second Form – of course everyone had been worrying about the possibility of war, since Chamberlain's visit to Munich the previous year and, to my eternal shame and sorrow, I was really excited about the prospect – still, I wasn't alone in this – many of my friends felt the same, but they didn't all have to pay the same price. Air raid shelters were being dug and constructed on every spare patch of land. Some of the playing fields were dug up at school and great, long structures – partly underground and covered with earth appeared. The people next door to us went in for an "Anderson Shelter" – about the size of an underground greenhouse. This was to save all their lives in 1941. We decided to trust in our complex of cellars. We had sandbags over the windows. We had a dormitory of beds – it was originally our washhouse so there was a sink with running water and I seem to remember a fireplace – we could really be quite comfortable.

Our part of the world was considered to be much safer than other big cities – so we were hosts to another secondary school – from where I can't remember. In fact, we never really knew our co-habitees because we used the school at different times. Each school had half the day – so sometimes we were there in the mornings and sometimes the afternoons and as the war deepened when we were at school we spent more and more time in the shelters. However, the early days – from September

1939 onwards it was all rather anti-climatic – the time of the "phoney" war – mainly remarkable in my family because my brother, John, married the girl next door – (not the next door neighbour with the Anderson Shelter). John had been born in February 1918 so in September 1939 he was 21 and one of the first young men to be called-up into the Army. He began his Army career as a Dispatch Rider and later joined the 51st Tank Regiment. His in-laws were called Davies. Mr Davies, a wee man, was a businessman somewhere in Liverpool – his wife, Maud, somewhat of a professional invalid (maybe I do her an injustice). They had two children, Maud Edith who liked to be known as Jaynie and Kenneth – a year or two older than me, whom I detested. After the wedding (there is a photograph somewhere in one of the big boxes) Jaynie followed John around the country in his various postings. She was a pretty girl, but immensely lazy and a poor housewife. I know my parents were disappointed because John had had so many girlfriends, many of whom they liked. The wedding day was a big event for me too. I wore a pinky-beige lace dress with a brown velvet sash and thought I was really something. I was 12. In 1940 Liverpool, like other cities, began to endure bombing – mostly at night – sometimes during the day – hence our time in the Air-Raid Shelter at school.

I must go back a little in time. In the summer before the war had began my father had found a good job working for a haulage firm, importing large bales of wool from Montevideo – hence known as "Monties.". He was working as a "Tally Clerk", checking the tallies on the bales with the loading lists whilst the bales, a tonne or so in weight, were manoeuvred onto big wagons taking them to woollen mills in Yorkshire. Tragically, one of these bales fell from the crane onto my father, crushing his poor legs. He was taken into the Liverpool Northern Hospital where the accident triggered yet another bout of Malaria – so he was very ill. At that time, children visiting were not allowed into hospitals so I remember, as a small child of 12, being dressed up to look older so I could visit my beloved Pop. This was the time when the submarine "Thetis", on its trial voyage, sank off the North Wales Coast with all hands. I remember my father's terrible distress as day after day, rescue attempts failed and all began to lose hope. It took a long time before my father began to recover from his accident and indeed he was still walking with two sticks for support in May 1941.

Around about the beginning of the war, my mother began to train as a Nurse with the Civil Nursing Reserve and it must have been about sometime in Mid 1940 when she agreed to go to Wrightington Hospital, near Appley Bridge as a full time Nurse. Things were becoming desperate in this field because of our war-wounded – although it was originally a sanatorium for Tuberculosis it was by now an Emergency Hospital. Many of the men being treated there were survivors from sunken ships – they had suffered starvation and immersion in salt water in the lifeboats for weeks or more at a time. Many of them already had incipient Tuberculosis and developed terrible TB abscesses and infected wounds. This time was just prior to the blessings of Penicillin and many of them developed Pulmonary TB and then TB Meningitis before dying – a heart-breaking time.

Our house was only two blocks away from the Army Barracks, so we were familiar with all the Bugle Calls, particularly the "Last Post". I can't remember when the Naval Transmitter Mast was installed but looking back it was clearly a moment of doom for my family. The Mersey then was full of shipping and all the docks were active. There would be ships queuing up all the way to the Bar Lightship to clear the channels and an equal number queuing up to get into the port. My brother, Alan, was then working in the Department to repair scientific instruments, so we were fortunate enough to have the odd gun-sight and binoculars to use. With these, we could see the shipping quite clearly from our top windows. Towards the end of 1940 we underwent some severe bombing. I was now becoming terrified at such times. The anti-aircraft guns along the beach between us and the sea were supplemented with mobile Ack-Ack guns which were at one particular time just outside the house. The Naval Mast must have been an important target because not only were the higher bombers dropping bombs fairly indiscriminately but other planes were flying lower and machine gunning, dropping incendiary bombs and anti-personnel bombs. I believe these had a long plunger mechanism which would detonate the bomb about head-height above the ground. On one terrible night, amidst all the pom-pom racket from these mobile guns – one of the anti-personnel bombs hit near a gun just down the road. My father, as usual, was on incendiary duty – trying to douse the fires before they got a hold. We were all in the hallway trying to get him into the safety of the house, amidst the terrible screams from the injured men. I was so frightened I thought my heart would burst. I don't know what happened to the poor men – my memory is very patchy at such times, perhaps blessedly so. What I remember is the acute panic and fear that we would all die then.

The months dragged on into 1941. John and Jaynie were in Colchester – his Tank Regiment preparing to go to North Africa – although we didn't know his destination. Ronnie was now 18 and opted for the Air Force. He had his call-up papers to go to the Training Camp at Padgate – somewhere near Preston I think – for sometime in the second week of May. He had been working for a Typewriter Firm in Liverpool, doing war work of course. Around the beginning of May he came home one day crying, carrying a birdcage. By some incredible chance, it was all that was left of the home of his friend at work – all killed, but the bird had survived. I don't known what happened to it. Time was now growing short for us. Heavy air-raids began again at the beginning of May. Ronnie and I had friends living around the corner – Dennis, Gwen and Gordon. My mother was of course away at Wrightington and on some nights when my father had to be on duty as a Fire Warden I would spend the night with Gwen in their narrow slit-trench of a shelter in their garden. On one of those early nights in May, when the ground seemed to be erupting all around us, we lay clasped in each other's arms, trying to claw our way into the ground. It seemed forever until Ronnie and Dennis arrived to comfort us.

Daytimes were spent in cleaning up rubbish, broken glass, swapping shrapnel fragments – preparing for the next night. All these days of May my mother had been becoming more and more frantic as she saw the bombing each night from the Hospital grounds. She could not get through to us on the phone so she somehow managed to get home. I think it was 6th May. She begged my father to come back to Wrightington with her but he was worried about the boys. "Wait", he said, "until Ronnie goes to Padgate next week then I'll find digs for Alan and then I'll come – but", he said, "you must take Pat". And that is how it was. The last time we saw him alive was on the Railway Platform, hobbling off on his two sticks as we set off for Wigan and then to Appley Bridge.

The digs my mother had were in a small council house – the home of Mrs Finch and her bachelor son Billy. It was generous of them to take me in as well. We had few possessions, mother had one or two changes of clothes as far as I remember, I only had what I was wearing. On the night of the 8th and 9th May, on reflection it may have been a day later, there was hammering at the door and a woman crying – Mrs Davies, our neighbour and John's mother-in-law. She brought to us the terrible news that all the others were dead. My father, Ronnie, Alan – her husband and son Kenneth, two spinster ladies at the corner house and one or two unknown persons. My God what a terrible night – poor Mrs Davies had been in the cellar with her cat beside her when the land mine fell on her. Planes carried two land mines – one under each wing and they fell quietly by parachute. She heard her husband and son in the hall above her shouting "Adolphs have got a direct hit". She was thrown half upside down with her head down – her cat beside her was crushed and she had to endure the agony of hearing her husband's cries to her getting weaker and weaker. The whole site was on fire and she was buried in the rubble for nearly 24 hours. Poor woman. My mother was almost destroyed – she wanted to die there and then – it was hard trying to hold on to her. She had the dreadful task of having to identify their bodies. The bombing had eased off by then and she and I travelled home. She had to go to the mortuary – my father had not been in the house, he had been fire-watching as usual. His body was found on the corner of the road – the cause of death – gunshot wounds. Ronnie was between the two big stone gate-posts and Alan had been in the cellar. Mother was only shown his hands to identify. Where our home had been was a great hole. Everything was plastered with a white deposit of ash – there was just a small stump remaining of the big sycamore tree in the back garden – that was the only landmark. There was nothing left but a few crushed pieces of brass, a half-burned book of fairytales and a silver-plated belt. Mother's nursing had now to become our only means of support instead of her war work and we had nowhere to live. My father had been 48, Alan 21 and Ronnie 18. Shortly after these events, John was sent overseas with his Tank Regiment eventually being part of the push from Alamein across North Africa to Tunis, then to Sicily and on to Greece. We were not to see him again until after the end of the war when he was demobbed.

I began school in Wigan at the Girls High School. I was a

desperately unhappy girl of 14. Lonely at home because mother had to work long hours – on days she left home at 6:00 am and returned at 9:00 pm. On nights she left at 8:00 pm and returned at 7:00 am. In time we rented two rooms in a house with a strange landlady. At school I was out of place – no-one there had had experiences similar to mine. I was a bit of a freak. I had no spare clothes, no background and bouts of tears. Eventually I made friends and settled down to work, but the scars never healed – they were only covered with thin skin.

My mother was an amazing woman. Despite her own pain – she tried to make life as happy for me as possible. Our time together was always quality time – she was artistic and graceful with a facility for making up verse – mostly amusing. She knew what it was like to be fatherless – her own having died when she was only two. She had a sister, Ella, 2 years older, and out of my father's large family we had only remained on friendly terms with his brother Bill, Bill's wife Dolly and young Bill. My mother was very wounded that none of them offered any help in our desolation and she was too proud to ask so we lost touch with them all for many years.

Pat wanted people to know how dreadful it was to live through air-raids which were terrifying as her account shows. To lose her father and two brothers, to have one married brother who was away and who she didn't know well, to have experienced poverty and to have survived left a scar and guilt, and she and her mother became very close. I think it left Pat with the resilience to survive but always conscious of her health. She had a fine intellect, a good memory and did well in school, enrolling in Liverpool University in 1945 and gaining a Batchelor of Science Degree in Botany.

She had been engaged to be married before she met Ben, who she met at a dance – a hop at the University, where he was a Dental Student. She and Ben had a lot in common, having both lost their fathers, they had an affinity and fun together as well as a deep friendship and love. They were married on the 21 December 1949 and on 2nd January 1950 Ben, who was doing his National Service, left for Egypt and Pat became a Teacher in Dronfield near Sheffield, teaching Science. When he returned and after he was discharged they bought a Dental Practice in Abergele in 1952. Sadly, her mother aged 62 years suffered a stroke and died at about the same time.

She and Ben had three children. Richard became a Scientist and is a Professor in Astrophysics, Nick a Dentist and Julia an Artist. They also made very good friends in the area and this period of her life was very happy. They lived above the Practice in a large comfortable house, Mor Awel, and between them created an imaginative garden with Pat's botanical plant-woman's skills and Ben's creative ability. Pat helped with the Red Cross and later returned to teaching.

At the age of 35 she became a Justice of the Peace and served on the Bench for 35 years. She became Chairman of the Bench for Abergele and Colwyn Bay, Chairman of the Juvenile Committee and also participated in the training of new Magistrates where she was strict but there her skills were rewarded by an invitation to a garden party at Buckingham Palace.

She was a Marriage Counsellor for a number of years, but gave it up eventually as she became convinced it was not helpful. She also counselled the Counsellors in a Children's Home. She was Founder and Chairman of the Abergele Abbeyfield Society, helping them to set up a house in the town.

She, Ben and Nick became very keen golfers and participated fully in Golf Club activities. Pat was a Past Lady Captain and also Lady President for two years. However, she became involved in a wider field with ladies golf and achieved a great deal. She was invited to become a member of the Ladies Golfing Union in the late 1970's and would regularly travel to St Andrews for meetings. Later on she became Chairman of the Welsh Ladies Golf Union. She had a lot of fun travelling with the International Golf Team to Norway,

Spain and Portugal. Her avid interest in golf continued even when she stopped playing. She also at some time learnt German. She and Ben had travelled to the USA many times to keep up friendships started in the Maxillo Facial Surgery Department at St Asaph.

Ben's death in 1989 was another blow for her after over 40 years of a happy married and fulfilling life. They had planned to leave Mor Awel and build a house in Bryn Twr on the edge of Abergele to their specification where again they planned to create a new garden. They had only just moved a fortnight earlier when he had a sudden catastrophic illness and died. She was left to cope with her new home alone. She had always been a scared woman – was scared of creaking floorboards in Mor Awel, scared of Ben's health after two heart attacks and was disposed to panic attacks, after which she gave up driving her car and had to be driven. She also hated thunder and fireworks, and slept with the lights and radio on. All this probably stemmed from her wartime experience and loss of family. The result was that her children and their families were very important to her. On her 80th birthday they had a weekend of family celebrations when she was surrounded by all her family. It was important to her also to ensure that they would keep together in future years. One of the joys of that weekend was that they made contact with John's two children after years of being estranged and after John had died and they all got on and enjoyed each other's company. The biggest influence which had blighted her life was the loss of her family in the war and it was a consolation at the end to find her family had come full circle and her children and eight grandchildren were close to her as were John's children and grandchildren.

She was a formidable, feisty, complex, argumentative and assertive woman who was strong on women's rights and could be militant in the Golf Club on women's issues. An avid reader she was good with crosswords and puzzles and a day or so before her death, whilst Julia and Nick were sitting with her and trying to find answers to a clue she opened her eyes and told them the answer.

Did she have ambition? She would have liked to have been a Doctor but family circumstances did not allow this, which was a disappointment but she took great interest in medical matters.

Fifteen years before she died she had Cancer of the Thyroid Gland and attended the Hammersmith Hospital for surgery and Radio Iodine and was cured, although she never fully accepted this. Eighteen months before she died she had a brain tumour and six months later developed heart failure. She was admitted to St Kentigern's Hospice where she had great care and remained mentally astute and alert until she died aged 81 years in a Nursing Home in Abergele on 24th December 2008. She was cremated in Colwyn Bay and the large congregation testified to the high regard in which she was held.

She was a multi-talented woman, a Scientist and a creative Artist having a good eye for colour and style in her dress and garden. She learnt massage techniques which she taught to others in the League of Friends of Glan Clwyd Hospital and in the Cancer Unit. She threw herself into community work on a voluntary basis and Julia wondered why she hadn't stretched herself to do a Ph.D. in Bangor University which she was certainly capable of doing. Was she satisfied with her life of being a good Dentist's wife and helping her community in so many diverse ways? Certainly, her married life and family gave her great happiness and she was pleased that they all got on so well together – a tribute to her and Ben. If there were disagreements she accepted them philosophically. The war left a permanent mark which probably increased the insecurity of her widowhood of almost twenty years.

If I had asked Pat what she had learnt from life Julia wasn't sure what her answer would be, but said that she felt strongly that women needed to be more assertive and view themselves in a positive light. And, if I'd asked of what are you most proud: she would undoubtedly have replied "my family".

Elizabeth Alice Jones JP [1940 -]
Wife of a Farmer and Charity Worker

Elizabeth Alice Jones, known to everyone as Alice, had known from a very young age that there was more to life than farm work and wanted to be part of this bigger world. She was fortunate that after her marriage and birth of her children the Chairman of St Asaph Hospital League of Friends, asked her if she would help her to start the League of Hospital Friends of Ysbyty Glan Clwyd and she became a Founder Member in 1974 before the Hospital opened in 1980  for patients. She became the first Rota Secretary and helped to recruit 500 volunteers to cover a rota for seven days a week of the Hospital Shop and Tea Bar. She was the Liaison Officer between the League and Hospital for eight years and was elected Chairman of the League 1988-1992, which was its heyday when people were happy to volunteer and be part of a network to form friendships. The shop was open-plan, and a disabled-friendly model, which with fund raising activities raised £1m in the first ten years. With help from sponsors whom she had cultivated when she was a Liaison Officer, the League raised money to fund a Pacemaker Theatre in 1995. She chaired two successful appeals to purchase modern machines – the Echocardiogram Machine in 1988 for the Cardiac Department and in 1990 the YAG Laser for the Surgical Department. They also raised money for further improvements to the ECG Department and Theatre Recovery Area as well as purchasing equipment for the Surgeons and Intensive Care Unit.

Alice was in her element with League activities. She had the support of staff and friends, and was able to combine bringing up her family, looking after a busy farming household and become a pivot for all the successes the League obtained. They were heady days with so many willing helpers wanting to back up their local District General Hospital. She retired from this active roll in 1992 when she became a non-Executive Member of the Glan Clwyd Hospital Trust Board and a Member of the Appeal Committee to raise £240,000 to provide accommodation for parents of the sick children who were patients in the Children's Ward. This was built by charitable donations from different sources, a donation from the Clwyd Health Authority, specific fund raising by the Committee and by local communities. A large donation was given by David and Vera Williams whose daughter had been killed in a road traffic accident and the house was named Tŷ Croeso Dawn Elizabeth House after her and opened in 1994.

Alice set up and recruited volunteers to form a PALS Support Group, to be a link with the local communities and fund raise to support a manager for the house and to provide a homely atmosphere during a stressful time for parents who wanted to be near their children. This house became a model for other hospitals to copy. Such was Alice's knowledge of the other voluntary organisations who supported the Hospital and the Trust that she was able to support and facilitate their activities also. In a reversal of her previous role as link person of the League of Friends to the Hospital she had now become the Trust Board Link with voluntary organisations and the community in the area the Trust covered, becoming Chairman of the Editorial Panel for "Tip Top" editing this newspaper covering 40 voluntary organisations.

In 1999 she was appointed to the newly reconfigured Trust of Community and Acute Hospitals which formed the Conwy and Denbighshire NHS Trust. She enjoyed her 10 years as Board Member and was Chairman of the first Equal Opportunity Steering Group set up by the Glan Clwyd Trust.

A Government-led campaign in the early 1990's wanted to ensure that by the year 2000 there would be more women pursuing careers in management, finance and business and there was to be emphasis on flexible working to enable women and men to balance their careers and personal lives. In 1995 the Trust won two prestigious All Wales Awards for their policies and was the first in Wales to appoint a dedicated part-time Equal Opportunities Officer. Alice was a member of the All Wales NHS Equality Forum and active in the progression of policies in equality and diversity in the Health Service.

A fluent Welsh Speaker she was the Chair of the Welsh Language Steering Committee set up to develop a Welsh Language Scheme which was formally adopted by the Trust in 1997 as required by the Welsh Language Act, the principle of which was to see that in the delivery of all services the Welsh and English Languages were of equal status.

She was a member of the Trust Charitable Funds Committee ensuring that public donations were invested safely, spent wisely and properly used for the purpose that they were intended according to the donor's wishes and for the benefit of patients. She retired from all these NHS voluntary activities in 2004, having given 30 years to help the Hospital, feeling it was time to move on. She enjoyed Glan Clwyd Hospital which was different from the Conwy and Denbighshire Trust. Michael Griffith (1934-2009) the first Chairman was excellent, he walked the corridors and knew what was going on. She felt she could give service, standards were high and she had a hand in things.

From 1993-2004 she was a Non-Executive Director of Clwyd Alyn Housing Association, and Vice-Chairman for two years. The Association provides social housing and affordable accommodation for vulnerable people, both young and old. It provides sheltered housing for vulnerable young adults, Group Homes, Care Homes and Extra Care facilities have recently been opened. She was upset by the stigma attached to social housing. "People don't understand it. It is unjustified and we need to raise standards and be

Ambassadors. If we don't do it, "who will look after the homeless?".
She thought Clwyd Alyn was well run by Graham Worthington, the
Pennaf Group Chief Executive, and his staff and it was a good place
to work. She was pleased in 2010 that this had been endorsed by the
Company being ranked within the top 100 companies, attaining a
national award in the UK for medium sized companies.

She was a Magistrate for 25 years, serving on a range of committees including Family Panel work and 15 years as Court
Chairman for the Youth Court. She was elected Chairman of the
Bench Training and Developmental Committee to lead and
implement a new National Scheme of Training and Appraisals for
all Magistrates. She was elected Bench Chairman 2006-08 becoming
a member of the Courts Management Committee and represented
North Wales on the Wales Bench Chairman's Forum. She also held
the position of Welfare and Social Officer for the Bench for many
years. She was elected Chairman of the Bench for a second term in
2008 but a serious illness from which she took some time to recover
made her realise that accepting a second term would be unwise and
consequently she resigned. She had represented the Denbighshire
Bench as a Committee Member of the Lord Chancellor's Advisory
Committee from 2002-2004, having been the Bench Representative
on the North Wales Probation Service from 1996-2001. This work
was demanding and its main role was dealing with criminal
offenders and their supervision within the community. They
undertake rehabilitation work with offenders and supervise ex-
offenders when they are released from prison.

In 1997 she was appointed a Member of the Social Service
Inspectorate for Wales who visit Local Authorities Social Service
Departments to review the standard of service provided to service
users. The Lay Assessor's role is to represent the voice of the public,
to ensure reviews are undertaken fairly and that the conduct of all
concerned in the process is respectful, honest and of the highest
standards. In 2004 she was appointed Chairman of the Care
Council's Registration and Regulatory Panel. This position is held

by a person who is independent of the Care Council. It involves setting standards for the conduct, practice and training of all social care workers in Wales. The Chairman is responsible for the conduct of hearings and ensures procedure is strictly followed when considering and making decisions about matters to do with registration of social care workers and allegations of misconduct against them. She completes her term of office in 2010 and is involved in the training of a new group of panel members.

She was born on the 23rd February 1940, a farmer's daughter, but her father also did a lot of Parish Council work, becoming Chairman, and she thought she would like to do something similar. She had ambition, knew she would have to study and had been taught the importance of family life and home skills even though they were of humble background.

She attended Prion School near Denbigh from 1945-1951 where she passed the Scholarship and went to Denbigh Grammar School, gaining 8 O' Levels and 3 A' Levels, winning several prizes and excelling at sports. She was in the school team for hockey aged 13 and became the Captain. She later played hockey with the Denbigh Ladies Team for several years. She went to Sunday School in Peniel as a child, walking three miles both ways. She trained in Yorkshire Training College of Housecraft, Leeds and gained a First Class Diploma in Domestic Science then proceeded to Leeds General Infirmary where she qualified as a Dietician.

She gained a post in Broadgreen Hospital, Liverpool, where she felt at home as the Nursing Staff were mainly Welsh or Irish. She had met Richard Jones, Pengwern Farm, Rhuddlan when she started college and this probably influenced her decision to return to Rhyl to the Royal Alexandra Hospital as Catering Manager/ Dietician. Her work entailed visiting the Royal Alexandra and War Memorial Hospitals in Rhyl and Chatsworth House, Prestatyn – a Maternity Home at that time, which later became a Community Hospital.

She married Richard in 1965 and supported him on Pengwern

Farm until he retired in 2007 when they moved to live in Llys Menyn, a bungalow they had built on the land. After 6 months of married life, she gave up her appointment in Rhyl and had three children, losing the middle one at birth. At that time married Farmers' wives didn't go out to work but she knew that eventually she wanted to return to having an interest outside her home.

It had been a big challenge being a farmwife on a big farm and rearing children – and also achieving her own things. To do it all she had to work long hours and be a good manager and organiser.

In her early years in Rhuddlan she had set up the first Welsh medium play school through raising the profile of its need and fund raising. This play school is still in existence. She became President of Bodelwyddan Women's Institute and Chairman of St Asaph Branch of Merched y Wawr and regularly competed and won prizes in agricultural and flower shows. She is a qualified judge of cookery, produce, needlework and handicrafts and has judged at the Royal Welsh Show. She also gave cookery demonstrations in various parts of the country.

In 1990 she became runner up from over 5,000 entries in a competition organised by the National Federation of Women's Institutes (WI) and sponsored by Calor Gas Limited of the "Citizen of the 90's" Award, having been nominated by Prestatyn WI.

In 2001 she was honoured with a Green Robe and made an Honorary Member of the National Eisteddfod of Wales Gorsedd of Bards. In 2006 she had two Awards – the Volunteer and Justice Award 2006 by the North Wales Criminal Justice Board and an Award by the Lord Chief Justice in recognition of 20 years service as a Justice of the Peace. She is still a JP, a Member of the Care Council and Chairman of the Independent Appeals Panel for Farmers.

She was appointed Chairman of the Independent Appeals Panel for Farmers in Wales in 2003 and reappointed in 2007 by the Department of Environment, Planning and Countryside of the Welsh Assembly Government, the only woman Chairman of the Panels. This process has been established to ensure that Farmers in

Wales who feel that the Department did not reach a correct decision on a subsidy claim have access to a fair and independent appeals procedure. Decisions are reviewed to ensure that the Welsh Assembly Government officials have been objective and applied the rules correctly in reaching their decisions.

She has achieved a great deal in her life and feels that she has succeeded against the odds as she has had a lot of illness. In her 30's she had Sarcoidosis which took 4-5 years to diagnose and treat. She lost a baby girl in labour and almost lost her own life due to severe haemorrhage but got over it - as she said "I pulled my socks up" and got on with it as there was no help available at that time to get over this type of bereavement, but as she gets older she misses having a daughter. She had a good relationship with her parents as they were a close family unit and were always at home. Life was hard for a woman on a farm as she grew up – a constant stream of washing and making food, but Alice has been lucky to have her sister Anne's support throughout her life. "You can't let illness master you – you have to be positive to get over it".

There are disappointments in life and she regrets that she was unable to go back to her profession, but feels that what she did was worthwhile and she has enjoyed it all. When I asked her what made her tick, she replied "challenges". She likes doing things and needs to have something to do. "Life is about doing. Look forward and have worthwhile projects".

She thought there was still a glass ceiling for women although not for her. "Women are bad at promoting women. Men promote men but men and women are poor at promoting women".

She thought women struggled when they were not at home to rear their children and the children could suffer. She thought women should stay at home until their children were of school age, not put them in a crèche to go back to work when baby was 6 months old but the cost makes this untenable, although the advantage would be a better society, because the social fabric would return. She feels a generation has missed out because of it. People are now asking "what makes a happy child?" – "having a parent with them". " Birth control came in with our generation". She said it had not been easy living in Pengwern amongst all the men, but she had been able to argue her corner and fight for herself.

When I asked her what she had learnt in life, she said "when you expect most in the volume of work you get least and when you expect the least you get the most". "Everyone doesn't want to "do" as its too much of a commitment".

Society has changed a great deal since she started her voluntary work. Mrs Roberts, Faenol Fawr, who had recruited Alice in 1974, was always addressed as Mrs William Roberts, not Olwen. Her husband was a JP, they had no children and he gave the land for the building of Glan Clwyd for the peppercorn sum of £10. Now people are referred to by their Christian name, although the tide is on the turn and patients are now asked what they want to be called. Manners are returning and are important.

"Are you a farmer's wife", or are you "the wife of a farmer"? There is a difference she told me: "Think about it".

Enid Wilkinson BA [1926 -   ]
Headmistress

When I asked Enid how she would improve life for women she at once said – "not by burning your Bra". She felt men and women should have the same opportunities "but we haven't got there yet". In every religion women are the lesser being and this is ingrained by society. People recognise there is a scale of difference between men and women. It isn't so easy now to have a baby, take 2-3 years off work, and

179

keep your place in your career. When she appointed women teachers she would ask during interviewing "what happens if your child is ill?", with a reply given "take time off". Enid would then point out the disruption caused by time off – it never occurred to the women to share time off with a man. "But they are not allowed time off". Enid thought this was unfair and the problem was "what to do with family life". Women can't give up their job as now they expect to have everything straight away and how to reconcile children, family life and careers has not been solved yet as changing our culture is very difficult.

What she has learnt is that the world needs tolerance of other people. Extremism is dangerous with only one right and only one Faith as in Catholicism. We should all be intolerant of the cardinal sins – greed, harming others, trampling over others etc.

When she was Headmistress of Beaverwood School, three incidents occurred which showed how much we need to improve for society to work.

The first was a formal Speech Day when she had invited Zoe Fairburn, a Novelist, as a Speaker. She was a Writer who ran Writers Workshops and was a Feminist. Speech Day for years had been stuffy with Governors sitting on the stage and at the end God Save the Queen being sung.

Zoe gave an excellent speech pointing out that marriage was not a bunker to hide away form the world but girls could have a career as well. Then she said she noted that they sang "God Save The Queen" at the end. She told them "I will stand, but I don't believe in God and I don't believe in the Queen".

SHOCK HORROR

One week later the speech was highlighted in the local press and the Governors summoned Enid to a meeting. "How had she chosen such a Speaker". The 6th Form girls thought the Speaker wonderful and why were the Governors so prejudiced and intolerant?

The second incident occurred some eighteen months later at the beginning of the summer term. The English Teacher had a serious illness and hadn't finished preparing the pupils in their set books for A-Level examination. She tried and failed to get a Supply Teacher and it was suggested she approach Mrs X who had just had a baby. Mrs X was a brilliant English Teacher, well known and respected in the borough, and when she agreed to help out the A-Level pupils in spite of the fact she was on maternity leave Enid was jubilant. She never thought for one moment that breastfeeding would become an issue! After all, this was an all-girls school and the four male Teachers made no objection. All the Teachers were of the opinion that their A-Level English students should be given every help to get their grades for their chosen Universities. A cubby-hole was found outside the staff room where Mrs X could feed her baby. This was also a time of Teachers Action when teachers didn't carry out lunch time duties.

All went well until one day a girl pupil saw the baby being breastfed, went home and told her mother who phoned the local press. The following week an article appeared "Head allows Breast Feeding in Class". Enid was inundated by phone calls including one from a features writer for the Guardian, who was not as well known at that time. This was a girls school, the baby had not been breast fed in the classroom – the whole incident had been blown out of proportion. Enid refused to comment. Was this more important than education? Do you want me to resign, she asked the Governors? One month later Malcolm was in a train going to a seminar in London, when he saw *The Sun* newspaper open on Page 3, always featuring topless models, with the heading "Breast Feeding in School reported in the *Johannesburg Times*". It saddens Enid that things have scarcely changed in the last 25 years. Men still see breasts as something rather prurient.

The third trauma she had had its basis in religion. In a daily assembly she had taken as her theme the 10 Commandments. Enid had studied the world religions and found they all had their ten commandments or truths. If they could all agree with and abide by these Truths it would be for the common good and there would be no wars. It was the law of the United Kingdom that every school should start with a communal form of Christian worship in the school. A complaint was made to the Governors that her Assembly was not Christian. When the Director of Education visited her she told him that she couldn't implement the law because the hall would only hold 500 pupils and she had 900, so it was impossible to hold a full Assembly every day. The National Association of Head Teachers (NAHT) pointed out that it was a problem for comprehensive schools to have a single Christian service. Enid was trying to make her pupils think in order to work with and tolerate each other as we haven't arrived at a single truth. She rang the head of the National Union of Head Teachers (NUHT) who told her to turn a blind eye and not to do anything. This law is still on the Statute Book and can't be implemented.

Prior to her marriage she had taught French in Hengoed Grammar School in South Wales where she wore a gown and had no problems. She didn't restart teaching until Sarah, her youngest daughter, was five years old and this in quite a different area – in Catford County in Inner London where one third of the girls were black and her biggest task was to control the class. The black girls were not on the whole the disruptive pupils. They were then in the 1960's fully integrated. Things changed after the Mexico Olympics when the hitherto peaceful Civil Rights movement led by Martin Luther King was highjacked by the Black Power Movement. They encouraged young blacks to assert their pride in their race and to fight against what they saw as the inherent "racism" of whites. From then on black pupils were encouraged to "stick together". This was, and still is, a very complex issue, the whole Black Power Movement being another example of how lack of tolerance on one side provokes an extreme reaction from the other side. When she entered the classroom she raised her voice to tell them to be quiet and told them that when she walked in and said "Bon Jour" they were to stand and reply "Bon Jour". One girl, Sylvia Freak said "I'm not b____ng well saying "Bon Jour". Sylvia Freak's answer to her request that they all reply "Tres Bien Merci" (very well thank you) to her asking them "comment Ca va?" (How are you?) was "Well I ain't Tres Bien, I got a bleeding awful cold." Her first lesson was to get her class to listen and to obey her.

In order for the girls to hear spoken French she organised a trip to France at a cost of £12.00 which covered everything. This would be achieved by paying two shillings and sixpence a week towards it. At a Parents Open Day she met Sylvia Freak's father who had said "no – it will be of no use for her to speak French when she is running my market stall in Lewisham when I've finished. "No b____ing use". Enid asked Sylvia to ask her father to attend the Open Day and he appeared in flashy jewellery and repeated "no b____ing use". Enid said "Think of it, Mr Freak, when the Channel Tunnel is open loads of French people will be coming to London, coming to your market and Sylvia will be able to talk French with them. It will be very useful and very good to get custom. In reply he said "'ere, take the £12.00. You may as well have the full amount whilst I'm in the mood". When Sylvia had walked down the gang-plank on their trip she had said with awe "I'm going to stand on foreign soil" - the first time she had done so.

Enid became very fond of Sylvia, but she left school before her O' levels. Eighteen months later the School Secretary told Enid there was someone who wanted to see her. "Who is it?", "Sylvia Freak". A smartly turned out Sylvia had broken away from her father, enrolled on a shorthand typist course and now had a secretarial post in County Hall. She had returned to say "thank you for encouraging me". Enid had encouraged Sylvia and all the girls.

Enid learnt more about teaching there than on any course. They were eye-opening years. She had one black girl called Cinderella and another whose middle name was Placenta. She thought it was important that Teachers should be exposed to all kinds of children of every race and every creed, and learn how to impart knowledge so that it is understood.

When Enid went back to teaching in the 1960's there was no "straight jacket" of a National Curriculum. Nor was it compulsory to have a Post Graduate Certificate of Education (PGCE). Now, 20 years after her retirement, no-one can teach without a PGCE and the National Curriculum has made teaching much more regulated and less of a vocation.

When the Headmistress in Catford unexpectedly died, her Deputy became Acting Head and Enid was nominated Deputy Head by the Governors, which didn't go down well with the older staff members who resented her. This gave her experience of administration.

She was asked to consider applying for the Headship of Rock Hills School, near Crystal Palace, but still in Bromley. It was a comprehensive school on two sites. The problems with Rock Hills School was not only was it on two sites but it was now a comprehensive school and a number of the staff were frankly not up to teaching a new all ability intake. Yes! It was a challenge! This school was looked down on by teachers in affluent areas as it was in the rough end of the borough and the two sites were 1½ miles apart, with the main Crystal Palace Road in between. It had been run as two separate schools which was not good. The Deputy Head was in charge of the old school and the Head herself, the new. There were a lot of problems and she had a week to decide. She told them she was not prepared to run it as two separate schools. It was going to be a poisoned chalice and tough, but she appointed good people and persuaded a lot of people to share the decision and take on a job. The problems were enormous and the Governors not helpful as they treated it like an old Secondary Modern School. It was a tough five years but at the end she was again summoned to Bromley and asked to become Head of Beaverwood School. The challenge when she took over Beaverwood five years later was the opposite; turning a Grammar school into a successful Comprehensive.

Enid believes in comprehensive education, but not the same scheme for everyone. She became a Head in 1981 and Bet, her mother, died in 1982. It was a big job and staff were difficult as they resisted teaching the less able, but one must not assume that children are badly taught in Secondary Modern Schools. Enid had thought of continuing until she was 65, but she had a scare with hypertension and she decided to go early at 60, as she had one crisis after another. She, two deputies and two dinner ladies had to supervise children's dinner hour every day as the children weren't allowed off the premises during the lunch hour at a time of industrial action. It wasn't helped by Kenneth Baker MP announcing that all Teachers and Doctors were interested in was what was in their back pockets. It was a difficult time and one day she became dizzy in the Staff Room. The Doctor was summoned, her blood pressure was too high and she was told not to return to school for at least two weeks. She and Malcolm had bought a house in Peterstow and that weekend Malcolm drove her there for a week. When she returned they had a long talk. She was due to have an increase in salary, but Malcolm said "to hell with money". She was tired, there was no point in pushing up daisies, never mind the pension. She retired at 60 and her blood pressure returned to normal and she realised how near she had been to a catastrophe. After Malcolm died it rose again, but she has learnt with medication and meditation to control it.

Both her Headships had been difficult. Rock Hills wasn't given a fair financial deal. The Borough gave finance to the affluent part and neglected the poor end and she felt this was an injustice. She needn't have taken either post, but didn't regret it. A new challenge was good.

The greatest influence on Enid's life, without a doubt, was her mother who was a strong willed feminist, keen on equality and education who lived by her principles. Enid's maternal grandfather was a farm bailiff of an Estate near Brithdir, Merionethshire and they lived in Hen Efail which is now the Green Keeper's Cottage of Dolgellau Golf Club. After his death in 1904 her grandmother with her six children had to move out of their tied home and they moved back to the family home – Fron Galed, Dolgellau. Ted, the eldest child, went to the Rhondda to find work, Gwladys went to London and died in her twenties of Tuberculosis. Cath also went to London where she met her future husband and they emigrated to South Africa. Crad emigrated to New Zealand before World War I but when war was declared, returned to fight with the Armed Forces, was wounded, met a Welsh Nurse, Gwladys in Hospital in South Wales whom he married and they later returned to New Zealand. The two youngest children were Bet and Ivor who remained with their mother in Dolgellau until Ted sent for them to live in the Rhondda with him. There was no widows pension and times were hard. She met and married a widower, a shopkeeper, Mr Thomas from Pembrey (known as Tomos Pembrey), who had two children and the four children were brought up as one family remaining friends until they died. This was a pooling of resources which was quite common after the early death of a spouse.

Bet went to Pentre Secondary School having won a Scholarship. Scholarships were given to ten pupils; boys and girls in the Rhondda, who had the best results at Higher examinations and who wished to go on to College or University after school. Her step-father supported this and wanted her to have every chance possible to improve her education. Enid's maternal grandmother had come from Newtown and when Enid was looking into her family history, she discovered that her grandmother had signed her Marriage Certificate with a cross. Her own mother had died young and she had to leave school in order to look after her siblings so she attached great importance to education and wanted her daughter to go to the best college. For this reason, and for her to broaden her education, Bet attended Reading University where she followed a degree course majoring in Geography. However, she didn't complete her degree as she felt she was needed at home as after two years, and before getting her degree, her step-father became ill so she returned to the Rhondda at the end of World War I and taught Geography in Pontypridd County School. She had excellent reports from her

Tutors and was given a Teaching Certificate. In Pontypridd she discovered that the female staff earned one third less than male staff and had hardly any free periods which she thought quite unjust. She was very proud that she had joined the march through Cardiff wanting equal pay for women, which they didn't get until World War II. This was where the seeds of Bet's feminism were sown.

The custom in the Rhondda during the "boom" years of the coal industry before the first World War had been for the colliers (as miners were then called) to give all their wages to their wives, who then gave their husbands "spending money". The story goes that on pay day, the women sat outside their houses, their aprons held out for the pay packet to be dropped in! As more "outsiders" came to work in the mines, the old ways changed. Going to the pub became more usual, although there remained a hard core of strict tea-totallers amongst the chapel goers. Roles changed and more men adopted the "English" way of leaving an envelope on the mantel-piece containing what they thought their wives would need! This did not go down well, and many men rued the day they tried to take control of the purse strings. Enid was amazed when they moved to Southeast England at the end of the 1950's, that most of her friends were not told how much their husbands earned. Her mother's words of advice to her before her marriage were "Insist on a joint account. What better way of demonstrating complete trust in each other!" Malcolm was in agreement. They never fell out over money.

Bet had a lot of courage to stand up for what she believed and this wasn't made any easier by her sister-in-law, Bopa May, and her opinions. Enid's father, Will, also a Teacher in the Rhondda had been to Brighton College – again to have a wider education. He adored his wife and supported her ideas. Enid said he sat back and smiled at his wife's crusades which at times must have embarrassed him at a time when there were few feminists in the Rhondda. Bopa May would try and interfere and point out "They say ..." He would not listen to any "tut-tutting" or "they say" and told her not to interfere.

When they got married, Bet had to give up her teaching post as married teachers were not allowed to carry on with their professions and she also had to give up being Captain of the Rhondda Girl Guide Company, which she had set up with Mair Davies (mother of John Davies, the Welsh Historian). This was a successful group and they would take the troop for farm holidays with the girls sleeping in the barn loft whilst they cooked the food below. She lost this because Baden-Powell didn't like married women as Guide Captains.

Soon afterwards she started a Girls Club in Treorchy and begged and borrowed a lot to help the Club which met on a Thursday night in the Cricket Pavilion on the same night as a "Seiat" (Prayer Meeting) was held in Chapel. The Preachers were against the Club's existence as they were afraid it would threaten chapel attendance, but none of her members went to Prayer Meetings or Bible Readings. In any case the Cricket Club would only let her use their pavilion on a Thursday. She stood her ground and Will helped her. She joined the National Federation of Girls Clubs which had access to books and formed a good library providing a valuable service to a deprived community. She would attend the Annual Conference of the Federation being taken there by the representative from Cardiff, who picked her up in her car. This again was a reason for tut-tutting – leaving her husband and children for a few days.

She and Will played golf from the early days of their marriage. People had got together and bought a piece of land to form a 9 hole golf course in Ystrad and planned the course which was unique, as golf seemed to be the domain of the well-to-do and they wanted to make Ystrad Golf Club a Club for everyone, including women. They set up a scheme whereby people gave old golf clubs to the Club so that Miners could use them. It was an example of socialism in action. It was at its peak in 1937, before King Edward VIII abdicated, when he toured the Rhondda, saw the poverty and announced "something must be done". Due to Ystrad Golf Club being unique he asked to visit it and her mother, two other women and two men were chosen to play two holes with him. A letter from an Equerry beforehand had specified that a new seat for the lavatory should be purchased and after the visit it was to be burnt – this they had to do. Naturally there was great excitement and Bopa May shared in this. Afterwards, she asked Bet – "Well, what was he like?" The reply: "a silly little man". Bopa May shocked said "you can't say that", the reply: "yes I can". She never talked about him afterwards. The King certainly didn't impress Bet. When war began Ystrad Golf Club fell apart because there wasn't the manpower to maintain it. There were no photographs taken of the Royal visit which Bet felt was a complete waste of time.

Bet with friends, also supported the opening of a Marie Stopes Clinic in the Rhondda as she was concerned about the size of families and the need for contraception and birth control. Before the war the Rhondda was a puritanical religious community who didn't believe in birth control and make-up was also frowned upon.

Before the war she and Will were involved in the Workers Educational Authority (WEA) and would attend courses in Coleg Harlech every August, the children being looked after by Annie – more disapproval. But it shows that Enid was brought up by parents who had a life together as well as being parents, through golf and Coleg Harlech.

Enid, and Bet especially, found the Rhondda claustrophobic. They both wanted to escape and holidays away were important. Bet and Will had a holiday in Switzerland before they married. Enid said holidays in the College Farm with us during the war was a life line for her with the freedom which we had. After her mother, Enid told me that my parents and Mamgu, my grandmother, Winifred Jones, were other big influences on her life. She adored my father who she thought larger than life and my mother and Mamgu very strong women. They were all very kind to her when she was recovering from Septicaemia and our holidays were a magical time.

I have known Enid (d.o.b. 22-12-1926), who became my best friend, for almost 70 years. Her father, Will, had one older sister who their family thought was a confirmed spinster and very straight laced, but who surprised them all in her forties by marrying my maternal grandmother's brother and widower of 65, as his second wife. In our family they were known as Uncle Davy or Uncle Defi and Bopa (Aunt) May.

In September 1940 the Battle of Britain was being won and schools were given 2 weeks holiday as the children had been kept at school in August. Will and Bet, with their family, were invited by my grandmother to have a holiday in Argoed, a farm in Cardiganshire. My father met the train in Aberystwyth to take them to Argoed and a few days later they were invited to our home so that we could meet our new relations. We all got on extremely well so it was decided that they should spend the rest of their holiday with us in Llangorwen. This was the start of our friendship and every year we spent a fortnight in Treorchy with them and they would return to spend a fortnight in the country with us.

Our holidays in Treorchy gave us a taste of the Valleys, of living in a terraced house, of Bethlehem Chapel, walking or cycling everywhere. In Cardiganshire, Enid and Betty, her sister who was 2 years younger (d.o.b. 22nd February 1929) sampled farm life, great freedom, trips to the beach by pony and trap, walking, swimming and riding.

Enid was educated at Porth County School and University College of Wales, Aberystwyth where she read French. Enid got on well with Professor Briggs who advised her to visit France and she exchanged a visit with a French speaking family in Belgium, who had a holiday home on the coast, north of Dunkirk. Her parents found the money to enable her to do this and said "make the most of opportunities that come your way".

In her first year in Aberystwyth, Professor Briggs had also advised her that there was a five day course in Somerville College, Oxford on Philosophy. The fees were modest and she, along with five others, were allowed to go which she found an eye-opener. She loved living in College and having a room lined by books. She had already questioned religion and found the discussion on the course stimulating and when she got home she announced she wasn't going to Chapel again. Although she got married there it was the last time she went. In spite of their views on religion she and Malcolm never considered marrying anywhere but in Bethlehem Chapel. The main reason was not to cause hurt to Enid's parents and especially Bopa May. In spite of everything she loved Bopa May dearly. She, along with thousands of other young women of her generation, was "left on the shelf" after the slaughter of so many young men in the First World War. She certainly became far less "judgemental" after she married Uncle Defi. Will said "Bopa May won't like it" and Bet said "it is nothing to do with her, Will" and there were no arguments. Bopa May thought "Nothing will come of girls being educated" and there were we: Enid – French, Betty, her only sister and me – Medicine. Her mother told Enid "be tolerant always".

She spent a year teaching in France (1947-1948) and on her return to Aberystwyth she gained Honours in French in the summer of 1949 and in August married Malcolm Wilkinson who had gained a 1st Class Honours in Chemistry and a PhD becoming a Research Chemist. She and Malcolm had four daughters, Ann in May 1950, Jill in July 1952, Jane in September 1956 and Sarah in May 1960.

Enid returned to teaching part-time in Catford in 1965, teaching French in the mornings only. She was then asked to teach Latin to the fifth form. She agreed to more teaching periods, insisting she had to be home by 3:00 pm to get Sarah from school. She agreed to teach until 2:30 pm every day and the time table was set to accommodate her.

Enid never had time to form attachments for she married young and had her first child in the first year of marriage. Her hands were full with her family, they were very hard-up and for the first two years they lived with Ma, her mother-in-law.

Malcolm and Enid were in rooms in Cardiff wondering how to cope when Ma, a widow, suggested she should sell the Florist Shop she and her husband had in Aberystwyth and buy a house in Cardiff and they could rent rooms from her so she would have an income as she didn't like the idea of them being in "rooms" when their baby was born. They moved in before Ann was born and Ma moved in later. Life for Enid and Malcolm with a new baby wasn't easy, neither was it for Ma for she missed the bustle of the shop. She liked nothing better than wheeling Ann in her pram to Albany Road where she soon became a valued customer to the good shopkeepers there, and was going through her capital at a frightening rate, they were not in a position to stop her. Bet and Will could see what was happening and told them that they would lend them a deposit for a house in Penybryn Road, Cardiff where Jill was born.

Enid didn't feel she'd had losses in her life : disappointments, yes, if she didn't get a job but she soon got over that. "Forget it" was her motto when Malcolm became upset about it. She felt she had been very lucky. Malcolm had never been ambitious and never asked for a pay rise so life wasn't easy and as they had four children she decided when Sarah was five to go back to work. They were always in debt, never having enough money, but all the children had the best start in life. It was difficult juggling home and a job, but she has been lucky with her career and has never had big cracks in her relationships.

Her biggest dream when young was to get out of the Rhondda as soon as possible and after she went to UCW Aberystwyth she never lived there again. She hadn't planned her life but felt that things happened to her and her parents understood. She became an atheist after attending the course in Oxford before she met Malcolm and nothing since has changed this, although she sometimes became frustrated as it was difficult to talk about it. Malcolm was always loyal to his family and family life was important to him. Enid felt that it was the way we behave towards each other that was important in life and the way to live.

192

When Malcolm died he was given a secular funeral and I was asked to give the eulogy – not a common occurrence then, but now more accepted. Peter, who is a practising Christian and Sarah's husband, didn't try to interfere and was supportive, letting his family make up their own minds. During her life Enid has not allowed disappointments to get her down but has put them behind her and moved on.

She doesn't believe in an after life but that the important thing is to make the most of this life. What matters today is what is important. During her teaching career she liked to get her pupils to think about Science and Religion, never suggesting that Science is the enemy of Religion. Having studied world religion she has tried to make pupils aware that almost all the worlds great religions have a great deal in common and it is only the extremists who have manipulated it to suit their own motives.

She has not been a driven person. She has had illness and has been fortunate with the attention and medication she has received. She is also fortunate, since Malcolm's early death (aged just 70 years), that she has been an independent person and been able to manage on her own for the last 14 years, becoming self sufficient.

Looking back over her career, she has appreciated her mother's wisdom in making her re-sit her Matriculation all those years ago. She was in no way ready then to make any sensible decisions about her future. Thanks to that year "out" she discovered that she had an aptitude for languages, especially French and Latin. From the former she has formed a deep attachment to France and French people, and it enabled her to experience a life changing year living and working in France in 1947/8. From studying Latin at degree level she became fascinated with the study of Linguistics, a subject which fascinates her to this day.

CONCLUSION

The women's lives portrayed in this book give a flavour of the life led by intelligent women who wanted an outlet for their talents outside the home. It is mainly an account of the contribution made by medical women to the development of the hospital service from the start of the National Health Service in 1948 to the opening of Glan Clwyd District General Hospital in 1980. However, the first four chapters give a background to women's role in Medicine, three have connections to Aberystwyth, three with Llangwyfan, three had sessional work in this area before the NHS commenced and one was my best friend in Medical School. They were all resourceful women, with eight having married and six having children. Her ethnicity had blighted one woman's life and illness altered the course of another two lives and choice of speciality.

I have included five married non-medical, intelligent, women with children in Chapter 13. The five had a medical connection, all had waited until their children were of school age before undertaking voluntary work or employment. One was proud that her mother had marched through Cardiff after WWI to get votes for women. Another tells of the blight on her life of the loss of family during the bombing of Liverpool in WWII. All five made valuable contributions to the communities in which they lived, and all felt it was important that mothers should stay at home with their children until they started school.

Most were born before 1930 and the youngest in WWII. Some learnt to adapt to changing circumstances on marriage and after they had children, finding different ways to utilize their talents and skills through openings which became available to them. Others remained unmarried. Women who became medical or dental general practitioners were not included.

It is no surprise to find that of the 13 medical women portrayed in chapter 5-12, who were working in this area from the beginning of the National Health Service to the admittance of patients to Glan Clwyd Hospital, eight were unmarried on appointment, five of these having been appointed as Consultants, three becoming Associate Specialists.

Only one was married on her appointment as Consultant and she came with her husband, both being appointed at the same time, their two posts fortunately having been advertised together. Two were certainly in their husband's shadow being known as Mrs Ivor Lewis and Mrs Parry Jones, neither of whom would have thought of coming to this area if they had been unmarried. One was a Consultant prior to marriage (Faux) and the other suppressed her academic side, her niche only becoming generally known on her death (Hampton). One, unmarried on appointment, later married but was unfortunately widowed after a few years (Frost m. Fogg).

Of the three appointed Consultant Physicians (Arnold, Emslie, McLean) all were unmarried, as was the Consultant ENT Surgeon. However, there were another two who were surgeons, one married with a Fellowship of the Royal College of Surgeons (Green) and another unmarried with no higher qualification in surgery (Roberts).

Five women who were married had children and another unmarried fostered a child for a time, before realising that the child would have a better future as part of a family. Another, unmarried, became a guardian of children of Missionaries. Only one of these women remained working as a full-time Consultant during her children's childhood (Faux).

It wasn't easy for women who married and then came to live in an area such as this, which was 40-50 miles away from a Teaching Hospital, to continue with their training once they'd had their children unless they were prepared to wait until their children were older. Jean Green knew that she would have to give up her ambition of becoming a surgeon when her husband attained a consultant appointment in Rhyl. Whilst Pat Barry was given a choice when Glan Clwyd Hospital opened, as the centralisation of many specialities made it feasible to apply for part-time higher professional training. A mentor was useful as one who had attained Consultant status told me. "Everyone needs a mentor with a carrot and a stick to spur one on", "Part–timers pack as much as possible into the time available".

It depends on the spouse and circumstances and adequate back-up help whether going back to work will be successful. "Don't expect the impossible, be patient and never give in".

Two, who became Associate Specialists gave up working completely until their children were all of school age (Rouse and Green). Both had four children and enjoyed family life, but wanted to return to their professional lives. One of these (Green) was given a Consultant session later to start a new service. Two, who were unmarried, had interesting lives (Padi and Roberts), failed to get higher qualification, yet made an important contribution to Medicine in this country and overseas.

One (Barry) changed from being a Registrar to a Clinical Assistant, taking maternity leave to have her children until eventually when Glan Clwyd opened she was able to continue her training, becoming a Consultant.

These women have a "get on with it" philosophy. Life is about "doing", looking forward and having worthwhile projects but everyone doesn't want to "do" as it is too much of a commitment. Although they felt that women need to be more assertive, they were also philosophical. "Don't expect too much of life and don't make instant judgements. Women should be negotiators". One wished society would find a way to help mothers stay at home if that was their wish. They also had a positive attitude to illness, a great love of life keeping them positive to overcome it. If they were bereaved it was felt they were better staying where they were, not running away but keeping their independence.

The arrival of two medical women in particular caused consternation to the male medical dominant fraternity of the time, who were expecting men to be appointed (Williams and McLean). Women were beginning to escape from male domination in the 1950's and 1960's and gaining lives of their own. Although, as is pointed out in Chapter 13, there was still an attitude of women looking for a doctor to marry as a bread ticket for the future. It was easier at this time to become a Consultant if one was unmarried, although for two (Arnold and Emslie) it took some time for them to arrange their work pattern to suit them.

These women did not think that there was a glass ceiling for women in Medicine, but there could be for women in low paid jobs. One told me that "she decided to study Medicine because she liked working with her head and her hands and Medicine, in particular Paediatrics, had given her a fulfilled life".

The National Health Service was a wonderful idea and the envy of the world, although Doctors were not used to the service they were to provide and pushed themselves to the limit work-wise. In those early days no-one minded working on a Saturday or Sunday. Many of the Consultants appointed to the area had been in the Armed Services and wanted the challenge of building a first class service for the future. Many of these male Consultants were sexist and didn't appreciate the contribution made by women in the workplace and thought a woman's place was in the home. There was consternation when a woman was appointed to a Consultant position. One medical woman felt her contribution was to work to serve the community and there was no time off. "As a female medic you have to cram in so much".

A career in medicine had something for everyone and one found on her retirement that nothing she did afterwards matched medicine for interest. Although they felt a mentor was important, it was also considered that "women are bad at promoting women".

The frustration that some medical women experienced in gaining a permanent appointment is chronicled as is the help given by the Medical Women's Federation in promoting schemes to retain women in Medicine and help them to return to Medicine.

We were seven Consultants appointed to this area in the 1950's and 1960's and I have portrayed the lives of the other six to give the reader a glimpse into a world where attitudes towards women were changing. These women had distinguished lives and were proud of the fact that they laid the cornerstone of services carried on in the First District General Hospital in North Wales. The work ethic was to serve the community which in today's world is rather an old fashioned attribute, but they were exciting times which we enjoyed. With the opening of Glan Clwyd Hospital attitudes changed with many doctors expecting more leisure to do other things and getting a better work/life balance. That is another story.

Phillida Frost, Buddug Owen, Nancie Faux

Hospital Medical Staff Committee outside Royal Alexandra Hospital, Rhyl – April 28, 1980.

Front row: Dr D Meredith, Dr C Hilton Jones, Dr M M McLean, Dr G Row (Vice-chairman), Dr B Owen (Chairman), Mr O Daniel, Dr J Alban-Lloyd, Mr E Parry Jones, Miss C M Williams.
Second row: Dr C Wright, Dr K Wright, Dr P M Frost, Dr G H T Lloyd, Dr E Emslie, Dr R Green, Dr J Arnold, Dr D A Jones, Mr E Lyons, Mr G Hardman. *Standing:* Dr Jamil.
Back row: Dr J Williams, Dr B Bhowmick, Dr D O Lloyd, Dr T Webb, ?, Dr D A Sutherland, Dr Viswanathan, Mr P Corkery, Dr A K Pal. Dr A Hampton. Dr P Needham.

Outside Royal Alexandra Hospital, Rhyl – April 1980.

Buddug Owen, Phillida Frost, Ellen Emslie, Catrin williams, June Arnold, Anne Sutherland.

Retirement Party of Dr Frost in 1988, showing the medical women in post before 1980.

Front row: Buddug Owen, June Arnold, Phillida Frost, Ellen Emslie, Nancie Faux, Muriel McLean.

Back row: Aileen Hampton, D. E. Jones (retired Deputy Administrator for Glan Clwyd Hospital), David Aiken (Obstetrician), Dr Ken Jones (Consultant Chemical Pathologist), Mike Hubbard (Orthopaedic Surgeon), Professor Robert Owen, Edward Parry Jones (Obstetrician), Edward Lyons (Ophthalmic Surgeon), Jean Green, Anne Sutherland.

Early 1990s – still together.
Aileen Hampton, Ellen Emslie, Jean Green, Phillida Frost, June Arnold, Anne Sutherland, Buddug Owen.

June Arnold, Buddug Owen, Ellen Emslie, Jean Green, Phillida Frost

ABBREVIATIONS

AA   Alcoholics Anonymous

AI   Amnesty International

AIDS   Acquired Immune Deficiency Syndrome

ARC   Rhyl Arthritis Club

ARP   Air Raid Precautions

CAFOD   Catholic Overseas Development Agency

CAMO   Chief Administrative Medical Officer

CC   County Council

CWVYS   The Council for Wales Voluntary Youth Service

DHSS   Department of Health and Social Security

DL   Deputy Lieutenant

ECT   Electro-Convulsive Therapy

ENT   Ear, Nose and Throat

FPC   Family Practitioner Committee

FRCS   Fellowship of Royal College of Surgeons

GCSE   General Certificate of Secondary Education

HSBC   Hong Kong, Shanghai Banking Corporation

LDF   Local Defence Force

MO   Medical Officer

MSc   Master of Science

MWIA   Medical Women's International Association

MWF   Medical Women's Federation

NAHT   National Association of Head Teachers

NGO   Non-Governmental Organisation

NUHT   National Union of Head Teachers

PALS   Parents Accommodation Link Support

PGCE   Postgraduate Certificate of Education

RAF   Royal Air Force

RAMC   Royal Army Medical Core

RNID   Royal National Institute for the Deaf

RRO	Ruthin Record Office
RSPB	Royal Society for the Protection of Birds
SOAS	School of Oriental and African Studies
UCH	University College Hospital
UCNW	University College of North Wales
UCW	University College of Wales
UN	United Nations
VAD	Voluntary Aid Detachment
WAW	Wales Assembly of Women
WEA	Workers Educational Authority
WCHMS	Welsh Committee for Hospital Medical Services
WCVA	Wales Council for Voluntary Action
WHO	World Health Organisation
WI	Women's Institute
WNC	Women's National Commission
WNSM	Welsh National School of Medicine
WRVS	Wales Royal Voluntary Service
WWI	World War I
WWII	World War II

REFERENCE LIST

Chapter 1
Blake, C —The Charge of the Parasols. Women's Press Limited, 1990
Brit. Med. Jr. —4th July 1953 pg.54. Colman – notice of death
Harris, N —Personal Testimony
Powell, D —*Liverpool Daily Post*, 7th March 2005 pg.10. Pioneering·doc dies aged 105
Price, N —Dorothea Colman. Personal Testimony
Roberts, A —The Welsh National School of Medicine 1893-1931: The Cardiff Years pg.143 Dr Erie Evans
Roberts, A —The Welsh National School of Medicine 1893-1931: The Cardiff Years pg.264 Dr A C Evans (University of Wales Press)

Chapter 2
Owen, B —Mary Angharad Guy: (The first woman doctor from Aberystwyth). Jr. Med. Bio. 12.1. February 2004, 201-214

Chapter 3
Morgan, M I —British Medical Journal, obituary 1976, September 11. pg.648
Ruthin Record Office —Mayer R. Von Stienen. Letter to Dr Biagi, Llangwyfan DD/DM/944/6
Hayward, E —British Medical Journal, 23rd September 1978 pg.904, obituary
Hoddell, C —Personal Testimony – E Hayward
Loxdale, HKR —Personal Testimony
Owen, B —A Rare Hero – Dr William Evans Gwasg Gee 1999

Chapter 4
Beer, W —A Portrait of the Caernarvon & Anglesey Hospital pg.93
Lancaster, D —British Medical Journal, 15th July 1961 pg.180, obituary
Lancaster, D —Jones O.V. The Progress of Medicine (1809-1948) Appx XVI Gomer 1984
Long, H —British Medical Journal, Vol 289, 28th July 1984 pg.258, obituary
Hughes —British Medical Journal, Vol 293, 1986 pg.569, obituary
Hughes, T —Eighty Years On Call 1971, Dragon Books, Bala

Chapter 5
Owen, B —Meeting Pioneers, Gwasg Gee 1994